£7.4?

Seeking Sabbath

My dearest Rachel,
I'm so sad to not live
across the road from you
anymore but I was so
blessed by that time, your
an amazing friend.
This book is written by the
principle of BBC, he's
quite wise for a Canadian
and I hope you can learn
something from this.
    Love you loads.
        Maurice
            x x x x

Published by
The Bible Reading Fellowship
First Floor, Elsfield Hall
15–17 Elsfield Way, Oxford OX2 8FG
Website: www.brf.org.uk

ISBN-10: 1 84101 536 9
ISBN-13: 978 1 84101 536 1
First published 2007
10 9 8 7 6 5 4 3 2 1 0

Acknowledgments
Unless otherwise stated, scripture quotations are taken from The New Revised
Standard Version of the Bible, Anglicized Edition, copyright © 1989, 1995 by the
Division of Christian Education of the National Council of the Churches of Christ
in the USA, and are used by permission. All rights reserved.

Scripture quotations taken from The Revised Standard Version of the Bible,
copyright © 1946, 1952, 1971 by the Division of Christian Education of the
National Council of the Churches of Christ in the USA, are used by permission.
All rights reserved.

Extracts from the Authorized Version of the Bible (The King James Bible), the
rights in which are vested in the Crown, are reproduced by permission of the
Crown's patentee, Cambridge University Press.

A catalogue record for this book is available from the British Library

Printed in Singapore by Craft Print International Ltd

Seeking Sabbath

A personal journey

David Shepherd

To Hilda

Acknowledgments

Because, for me, the very act of writing incurs a debt of gratitude, the following expressions of thanks can only begin to repay what is owed. I am very grateful indeed:

To those Jews and Christians over the centuries who have sought the sabbath themselves and been willing to share something of their experience with the rest of us.

To Colleen and Cal for reading an early draft of the manuscript, and to the rest of the faculty at Briercrest College and Seminary for their scholarship, friendship and fellowship during my four years there.

To Naomi and the rest of the folks at BRF for the kind of sense and sensitivity in equal measure that make publishing a truly pleasurable experience.

To the members of First Free Methodist Church, Moose Jaw, Saskatchewan, for opening up their hearts and their homes to us as we worked and worshipped together during my time at Briercrest.

To my parents, for ensuring that my experience of sabbath as a child was not merely memorable but also worth remembering.

To my girls, Anna and Sophie, and my wife, Hilda, for putting up with my 'projects' and patiently reminding me of what is truly important in this life.

Prologue

Perhaps it makes sense that the longer something has been lost, the harder it seems to be to find. And if that something is lost for long enough, we may forget that it exists, if only we would begin to look for it. The fact that the sabbath of my past had not slipped altogether beneath the murky surface of my memory is perhaps not entirely surprising, though. As a Christian, I still went to church on Sunday and, as a lecturer in Old Testament at a theological college, I regularly took my students through passages that had plenty to say about the sabbath. And yet, in the midst of it all and almost in spite of it all, it occurred to me one day that at some point, the sabbath I had once known well and still did in theory had somehow been lost to me for all practical purposes.

As with most things that are lost, it was impossible to say with complete certainty when it happened. Appropriately enough, it may have been around the time I began to work. As an undergraduate student in Canada and then especially as a postgraduate student in Scotland, remembering the sabbath was simplicity itself, for there was neither cause nor need to forget it. After all, there were few books so significant, few essays so demanding, that they could not quite easily be put off until Monday. With a rented apartment, only a bicycle to maintain and merely myself to look after, the question wasn't whether I should take Sunday off, it was whether I shouldn't take Saturday and perhaps even Friday as well.

Things began to change when I finished at Edinburgh University and began to work at St Paul's and St George's—a church in the centre of the city which was full of wonderful people and marvellous ministries, many of which took place on precisely the same day they would at any other church. Although I had heard it before, it was here that I learned for myself why those who proclaim the importance of the sabbath often have the hardest time keeping it themselves. For quite different reasons from when

I was a student, the question wasn't whether I should take Sunday off, it was whether there would be any day off at all in the midst of a weekly calendar that was rewarding but also utterly relentless. Despite my own best intentions and those of the Rector who supervised me, my sabbath began to slip away—or perhaps it's more accurate to say that I began to put it away. On my weekly day off, I would enthusiastically pull out the idea of a day of rest, admire it and perhaps even remember how much I'd enjoyed it in the past. But as I did so, it wasn't long before I was remembering other things, most of which would have to be done before the coming Sunday. And with that, the idea of the sabbath would be shelved for another week, or perhaps, I began to think, another life.

If the sabbath that had begun to slip away had been mine alone to lose, at least I might have been the only one suffering. But a day of rest was one of the many things my wife Hilda and I shared as we began married life together in Edinburgh that same year. Unfortunately, with her working during the week and me at the weekend, it was one of the few things that we gradually came to share less and less. As my sabbath began to disappear, so did hers, because, of course, two cannot share what one cannot keep.

When 'another life' came along in the form of a teaching appointment in a theological college back in Canada, not far from where I grew up, I somehow thought that things would be different, that a day of rest would be easier to find. We were, after all, moving to a place called Moose Jaw. In a province with as few people as Saskatchewan had, Moose Jaw was officially a city (population: 30,000; moose: 1) but essentially a town. Having been born and raised not far from Moose Jaw, I knew it was the kind of place where things moved at a different pace, the kind of place where the worst traffic queue was in the doughnut shop drive-through, but most importantly the kind of place where I was sure I'd recover what remained of my sabbath.

I was wrong, of course, for reasons that many first-year teachers will understand all too well. When you're staying just one page ahead of your students and you're teaching on Monday, you often end up working on Sunday. In that first year, the idea of sabbath didn't need to be put away on a weekly basis because I never managed to drag it out in the first place. Like many of the things we brought to Canada, which were left in boxes in cupboards or the basement, the idea of a day of rest remained in storage that first year, packed up and hidden away somewhere. The second year was a little better—but only a little. Instead of staying one page ahead of the students, I was ahead by two, but by then my sabbath had been stored away so long that I wasn't quite sure where to look for it. And even if I had known where to look, I wouldn't have had the time to do so, with sermons to preach and papers to mark and more new classes to prepare.

When I was asked to become Dean of the college a few years later, life suddenly became even busier. On top of teaching, there was now a faculty to develop, a curriculum to plan, partnerships to nurture, and even less time to observe a sabbath which was long forgotten anyway. The passing of each Sunday was, of course, a reminder that the sabbath was around there somewhere: like so many other unused things in my basement, I would never have thrown it out. But, like those same things in my basement, I might as well have done for all the good it was doing me and for all the glory it was bringing to God.

And then, one autumn, something began to happen. I began to remember. Precisely when it started, I couldn't say, but it was around the time of our faculty retreat, before the arrival of the students. Somehow the conversation turned to the sabbath as we shared our memories of what it had meant for each of us, growing up. When someone asked what the sabbath meant for us today, however, the conversation began to dwindle perceptibly and then it seemed to die altogether. Apparently, whatever the sabbath had meant for us in the past, today it didn't seem to mean much more to the rest of the faculty than it did to me, and it left me wondering why.

By the third week of term, the faculty retreat seemed a distant memory, almost as if we'd gone not the previous month but the previous year. Welcoming the new students, answering questions from all quarters, implementing new policies and, of course, the inevitable seemingly interminable meetings had all begun to take their toll. At church, they were asking if I would teach a Sunday morning adult Bible class. At home, we needed to sow a new lawn before the ground froze in the coming weeks. I felt hurried and harried and it wasn't even the end of September. In the midst of it all, I was teaching the Torah, and as we moved through the first five books of the Old Testament we happened to land on the subject of sabbath. We discussed the fact that while Exodus instructs the people to 'remember' the sabbath day (20:8), Deuteronomy requires them to 'guard' it (5:12, author's translation). As we talked, I was reminded that I had long since stopped doing either. Far from guarding or keeping the sabbath, I wasn't even able to remember the sabbath. To remember the sabbath, you first have to remember where you left it and, if I was honest with myself, I had to admit that I didn't.

So I decided to do what most of us do when we want to find something that's lost. I decided to start looking for it—not because my theology required it (however much my parents' might have done), and not because I was contemplating conversion to Judaism, but because, with a few exceptions, the idea of a day of rest, first for Jews on Saturday and then for Christians on Sunday, had done more good than harm for God's people. Thanks to my understanding of what Christ had done on the cross, I didn't start looking for the sabbath because I feared that my salvation was somehow at stake, but because I had begun to suspect that my sanity might be. In the midst of an overwhelming tide of work and worldly pressures that threatened to sweep away all before it, what prompted my search for sabbath was a very real sense that my life depended on it—not the life hereafter, but simply the life here and now.

Having decided to search, the next question was how to begin. I decided to take Exodus at its word (at least, at one sense of its word) and begin by remembering. I was, after all, hardly the first to go in search of the sabbath. Down through the ages, first Jews and then Christians had not only accumulated considerable experience at keeping the sabbath, many had also spilled considerable ink to document their efforts. Although my memory would need to be selective, I wanted to search for the sabbath by looking back and learning how the tradition to which I belonged, from the prophets to the Puritans, had sometimes made a mess of the sabbath but had also, more often than not, made the most of it.

At the same time, I wanted to remember a more recent past. I wanted to remember something of the sabbath I had experienced growing up in a Methodist family on the Canadian prairies. I wanted to remember back to a time when losing the sabbath seemed as unthinkable as forgetting to breathe. I could not return to that time, of course, for there is no going back, but I might remember what it meant then and realize what it might mean now to set a day apart.

I also recognized that if I was going to rediscover the sabbath, I would need to do more than simply remember. If, by 'remember', Exodus means something like what we mean in English, it also means something far less cognitive and far more active—something, in fact, very much more like Deuteronomy's instruction to 'observe', 'guard' or 'keep'. Having lost the sabbath, it became clear that the only way for me to find it again was simply to begin to keep it in whatever way I could.

After discussing it with Hilda, I made a decision: For six months I would seek the sabbath by deliberately reclaiming Sunday and setting it apart. The sabbath of my childhood memory began on Sunday when the sun came up. At least, it did in theory. In practice, it began as late in the morning as possible and, much to my father's chagrin, often right around the time we were meant to be leaving for Sunday school. Because Sunday was a school night, sabbath was effectively over after evening church, and even when I got older and my bedtime got later, the sabbath seldom outlasted the daylight by much.

When I was in Jerusalem, where I spent a summer during

my university days, I discovered that the difference between the *shabbat* of Jerusalem and the sabbath of my youth was not just the day but when the day began. According to the rabbis, *shabbat* begins at sunset on Friday evening, but, as any unsuspecting visitor will testify, in Jerusalem it begins well before. By three in the afternoon, some Jewish shops are already closing, and within the next few hours the rest follow suit. If they don't, it doesn't matter much anyway, because without the buses they are rather difficult to get to. By sunset on the sabbath eve, silence has descended on Jewish Jerusalem as the faithful file into the city's synagogues, and it is only when the sun begins to slip beneath the Mediterranean on Saturday night that Jerusalem begins to bustle again.

In our part of the world, though, tying our sabbath to the sun instead of our supper would have meant celebrating nearly two sabbath days during the summer and half of one, if we were lucky, in the winter. For Hilda and me, a sabbath that stretched from supper-time on Saturday night until the same time on Sunday seemed best, not only because it was the baby's bedtime but also because, by Sunday evening, my mind was often straying to Monday and the week to come.

What you will find in the pages that follow is the story of my search for sabbath, a story written in conversation with the great story of our forefathers in the faith. The fact that it is neither purely exegesis nor only exposition of the biblical sabbath is a reflection of my feeling that others have already produced much of both, to the glory of God and the benefit of his people. What follows is instead a personal exploration of what it meant for me to seek out a sabbath that was long lost, yet not lost so long that it was beyond remembering. Because I have written it down and been persuaded to publish it, it is my hope and prayer that this recollection might also be, in some sense, an invitation to you not merely to share my search for sabbath but to seek it out for yourself.

✝

Learning from the geese

Our first sabbath began with Burger King. Having spent the better part of Saturday doing nowhere near half the things we had planned, neither Hilda nor I had the energy or imagination to summon up supper for anyone apart from the baby. Quite the opposite of the Jews of Jerusalem, we'd worked right until the last minute, only to collapse in front of the television and watch a movie that would have been scary if it hadn't been so frighteningly bad. It was only on the next day that I wondered whether relying on someone else to cook your supper so that you wouldn't have to was really much of a way to remember the sabbath.

After an unseasonably cold August, we were enjoying an Indian summer, and after church the next morning we decided to have our lunch under the trees on the deck at the back of the house. After we'd finished our lunch and while Hilda was feeding the baby, I noticed that the deck and the lawn beyond were strewn with leaves that had fallen during the night. Surely raking leaves was allowed on the sabbath, wasn't it? Perhaps because she'd done it every day that past week, Hilda informed me that for her it definitely was not. For me, on the other hand, it seemed a refreshing change of pace from marking essays, so I picked up the broom and eventually the rake and tidied up the garden. Already I was beginning to understand why the rabbis had a hard time agreeing about the sabbath. While Hilda and I didn't agree on the raking, what we did agree was that on a day like this we should spend our sabbath afternoon out of doors and in the midst of God's creation.

The rabbis warned against walking too far on the sabbath, but it was pretty clear that the best way for us to keep the sabbath as a family was to keep me as far away from my desk as possible. So we packed up the buggy, filled up with fuel and headed toward the country park half an hour north of where we lived. Not far outside the park gate, we passed through some pasture land and, as we did, just beyond the ditch to the right of the road, a herd of cattle caught my eye. It wasn't so much what they were doing that caught my attention as what they weren't doing. In fact, as far as I could see, they weren't doing much of anything at all, apart from sitting in the grass, basking in the sun and swishing their tails when the spirit moved. Exodus reminds the Israelites to allow even their oxen and donkeys a sabbath, but it hardly seemed that these cows needed any reminder to rest. As we sped by, it occurred to me that rest seemed to come quite naturally to them in a way that it hadn't to me for a very long time indeed.

A few minutes later, the road dropped down off the plains, descending into the valley before turning to run the length of the lake. Eventually, pavement gave way to gravel and we soon found ourselves near the end of both lake and road, which I knew meant that a walk was inevitable. It was not that I had a problem with walking. I walked all the time: from my house to my car, from my car to my office and sometimes even back to the car again if I had forgotten my break-time soup on the back seat. Unlike Hilda, who loved nothing more than stretching her legs down some path or lane, I saw walking as essentially a necessary evil, a last resort. It was what you did when your car broke down, or when it came to the end of the road, as ours had now.

The path we walked led us out of the rolling hills and golden grasses of a prairie water's edge and into the marshland beyond. As we strolled along the boardwalk among the bulrushes, I heard the distinctive call of the geese and looked up to see the sky full of their familiar formations, wing to wing, and in great squadrons. They were doing what many of us would have, if we could have. They were flying south for the winter. I learned that the marsh through which we were walking was part of that journey, a resting point along the way for the thousands that make the same trip every autumn. I wondered idly what might happen to them if they decided not to land here one year or stop at other regular points along the way. I knew nothing of migratory birds, but decided that they probably wouldn't make it, wouldn't get to where they were going. Of course, for a goose to do that would be silly. Only a silly goose would attempt to make a journey like that without taking regular breaks along the way.

Our way home took us back through the pastures and into good grain land. A week of warm weather had finally given the farmers a chance to begin to get the harvest in, and what wasn't already in the barns lay in the stubble in great long lines. Having given of itself since early spring and all through the summer, the ground itself was ready for a rest—ready to take its well-deserved break along with the men and women who worked it from sun up to sun down.

In Exodus 20:11, we read that God set apart a sabbath day because he'd taken one himself after he brought forth creation. As the city drew ever nearer and we left the harvest fields behind, I became convinced that creation and its Creator had conspired against me—conspired to remind me that if I wanted to find the sabbath I was seeking, I could do worse than to learn from the geese.

+

Merciful miscalculations

The next weekend, in the very same service as my Quaker wife was
to be granted membership in our local Free Methodist Church, she
and I were also bringing our 10-month-old daughter to be dedicated, as all good Methodists do in North America. To celebrate
this unlikely convergence of commitments, we decided to invite
my immediate family, and a few of the less immediate but more
likable ones, to come to the house for Sunday dinner.

At least, that's why most of them were coming. For my dad, I
knew that the dedication and even the dinner were little more than
a pretence, little more than a socially acceptable excuse to whip my
house, garden and garage into shape yet again. Not that I minded,
of course. In fact, I encouraged it. Hilda and I agreed that my
father's power tools and his pathological hatred of anything un-
tidy, unpainted or unfinished were the only thing that kept our old
house from falling apart.

To no one's surprise, my parents decided they would drive the
two hours from their house to ours on Friday evening in order to
get both a good night's sleep and an early start the following day.
My father reminded me that before the baby could be dedicated,
there was a new set of steps to be built at the caravan—bought in
a moment of madness when we'd arrived in Canada. Wilting at the
prospect but unwilling to stand in the way of progress, I gathered
together the materials and my meagre assortment of tools and we
arose early the next morning to set to work.

Work was one of the things my dad did best. At least, for the better part of my childhood it was what I remembered him doing most. I can only imagine that, as with most workaholics, it must have begun innocently enough. As a young man, he'd probably started working a little just to relax after he got home from… well, work. But before he and we, his young family, knew it, Dad seemed to be working all the time. Sometimes he'd work with friends and family, but most of us found it hard to keep up and he would often find himself working alone. Whether it was at the office or around the house, it began to seem as if he needed to be working to have fun. Eventually, of course, as addictions often do, his constant working started causing problems at home and in his relationships, but it was only when working itself became difficult, when he had to stop work altogether and seek help, that he realized that he had developed a working problem. Ever since, Dad had been a recovering workaholic. Unlike alcoholics, who can never go back to drinking, most workaholics eventually go back to work, and so did my dad, but from then on he worked a little less and played tennis a little more.

For me, though, the damage had been done. The gene had been passed. At some point along the way, I too had become a workaholic, and although a part of me knew that I needed to rediscover the idea of rest, another part of me wanted those steps done before we stopped for the day as much as my dad did. Although I'd resolved to begin my sabbath each Saturday at supper-time, I also remembered that in order to squeeze every last workable second out of his Saturdays, Dad would often work late into the night. He'd driven all the way down from the city to help me, and as he unpacked the floodlights he assumed we'd be needing later on, I realized that the only way we could avoid needing them was if I worked much much harder than I thought I could. I also knew that it always took longer than we expected for Dad and me to do things like this—and so it did. As the shadows started to lengthen and the air began to cool, it became clear not only that the sun was about to go down on my half-built steps, but also that I really would have to say something soon. When I mentioned that I wanted to stop around supper-time, my dad was a bit surprised. Why, he wanted to know, was I starting my sabbath at the Jewish time instead of the Christian? When I explained that I wanted Saturday evening to be the beginning of my rest and Sunday evening to be the beginning of the week's work, he didn't necessarily agree but I saw to my relief that he did seem to understand.

Only after we'd agreed to finish without being finished did we realize that time wasn't the only thing we were running out of. We were also running out of wood. In my frantic preparations for our project the previous day, I had paid a visit to my local timber yard. As I had done on countless occasions, I had placed my order, paid my bill and headed round the back to collect my wood. I had carefully counted the twelve planks as the man had loaded them and then again when I unloaded them. But as we got down to work and the planks went down, it eventually became clear, first to Dad and then to me, that we weren't going to make it, not with the number of planks I had bought. Why I ordered and loaded twelve planks when I knew perfectly well that we needed 16 to finish the steps, I'll never know. Perhaps I was just in too much of a rush. But perhaps there was a bit of God's mercy in my miscalculation. With the timber yard closed, we couldn't get any more wood, and without wood there would be no more work that day.

As we packed up the tools, I reminded myself that there was no reason whatsoever why those steps needed to be done before the baby could be dedicated. I reminded myself that what we had done on the steps would still be there after the sabbath, and that what we hadn't done could and would be done another day. As we walked into the house, it dawned on me that after a day full of work, what both Dad and I needed most of all was not the satisfaction of finishing the steps but the chance to relax over a bite to eat before turning in for the night.

10 October

Finding time for the rest of the week

Unlike our neighbours to the south, Canadians apparently can't wait for Thanksgiving. Just as well, then, that it comes to Canada a month earlier than it does in the States. In our family, we always gathered at my parents' place, so the following Saturday found us driving up the same road they had driven down the week before. Along with Christmas and Easter, Thanksgiving was one of the occasions that drew the extended family on my mother's side together for what Dad liked to call a 'family horror show'. The cast assembled for these shows was invariably large, the lines delivered invariably loud, and the menu almost always luxurious. For me, the scariest part of these productions was that no matter how much food was brought, by the time it was all over, there was rarely much left.

This year, the festivities weren't to begin until mid-afternoon on Sunday, and as we lingered round the lunch table, I surprised myself by suggesting a walk. While the idea was greeted enthusiastically by the women, the men around the table seemed notably less taken with it. My brother-in-law said that he'd rather go and work on the house that he and my sister had recently bought and were now renovating. When I told him about my sabbath experiment, he said that, for him, working on the house was fun—so much fun, I discovered, that for the last seven days he had come straight home from his day job in order to work on it. As a recovering workaholic, I was pretty familiar with this line of reasoning. I'd used it myself countless times. But when I saw how exhausted my brother-in-law looked, I wondered whether all this fun wasn't beginning to take its toll. I wondered whether fun was necessarily the same thing as rest, and whether the rest of his family was having as much fun as he was. The look on my sister's face suggested that perhaps they weren't.

One member of the family who was certainly interested in a walk, however, was Harley, their new dog. According to Jewish tradition, dogs that usually fetch the paper don't have to do so on *shabbat* because even they deserve a day off. And on this day, Harley led the way down the path that ran along the river. Later, we returned from our walk to find the house abuzz with preparations and, before we knew it, full of people... and pie. This year, aunts, uncles and cousins of all ages had been instructed to bring plenty of pies and that's exactly what they did. As the house filled with people, the table in the kitchen steadily filled with pies and pastries of every description. Mum's lemon meringue, Auntie Libby's peach and Auntie Colleen's apple were soon joined by pumpkin, raisin and several more exotic fillings as delicious as they were mysterious. For traditional Judaism, of course, the sabbath has long been a day of fellowship and feasting. The Talmud teaches that because the Hebrew word for 'day' appears three times in Exodus 16:25, Jews are to eat three square meals on the sabbath, even when, during the rest of the week, they would normally eat only two. If, as one of the rabbis taught, those who eat all three sabbath meals will be spared the suffering of the end times, then the apocalypse should hold no terrors for my family.

Later on in Exodus, God tells his people to keep the sabbath 'throughout their generations' (31:16), and as I wandered through the house amid the barely controlled chaos of some rooms and the quiet conversation in others, it occurred to me that just as my childhood experiences of the sabbath were due in no small part to my parents, so too were the previous generation's. My grandparents on my mother's side were staunch Free Methodists and although the denomination claimed to be free of all sorts of things that plain old Methodists weren't, they certainly weren't free to do much of anything on the sabbath. My mother and her sisters and cousins had vivid memories of sabbath-keeping as children. For them, the Lord's Day was, as it has been for many down through the ages, a day of 'do nots'. The rabbis themselves list 39 things that one shouldn't do on the sabbath. Although the Free Methodists of my mother's generation didn't have quite that many, they did have their fair share and, it seemed to me, several more than seemed necessary.

One thing you didn't do on the sabbath was to play with a skipping-rope or bounce a ball—unless, of course, each skip or bounce was accompanied by a book of the Bible: 'Genesis—Exodus—Leviticus—Numbers... Deuter-Onomy—Joshua—and Judges.' Another thing you didn't do was to buy anything on the sabbath. So deeply and indelibly was this rule etched on the minds of my mother and her sisters that their teenage memory of someone offering to buy them ice cream on the sabbath was one not of delight but of guilty indulgence.

Then there was the time when the young man who was courting my mother's eldest sister (and would later marry her) had hitchhiked up north for a weekend visit to my grandparents' home. When Sunday's arrival heralded the young man's departure and he prepared for the journey south, my grandmother insisted on packing him a lunch. As she began to do so, however, she discovered to her dismay that what little bread they'd had left from Saturday was gone. The staunch Free Methodist family faced a dilemma: keep the sabbath and send the boy south without a lunch, or break with tradition, buy a loaf of bread and send him off with a sandwich. With the words of the Gospels ringing in their ears, the family decided that the bread should be bought and the boy fed.

The irony is, of course, that of all the Ten Commandments, the one about keeping the sabbath is the only one that tells the people of God what they should do instead of what they should not. This is perhaps partly why, despite all the 'shalt-nots' of my mother's childhood, the sabbath remains in her memory as a treasured time—a time for family and, above all, a time for rest. For her family, the sabbath was in a very real sense the 'rest' of the week, because the 'rest of the week' was full of work, of a sort that was more demanding than what some of us do today. In those days, after a week of hard work, what the family needed above all else was a 'rest', which is why, in my mother's house, Sunday was the one day of the week when anyone and everyone could indulge in the traditional afternoon nap—a custom practised daily by our Latin American neighbours to the south but neglected by us in the north.

I had long since mastered the art of falling asleep in front of the television every night, but I couldn't remember the last time I had had 'a rest'. That Thanksgiving day, full of pie and feeling drowsy, an afternoon nap suddenly sounded like one of the best ideas I'd heard in a long time. As I looked up from the dining-room table where I was sitting and glanced through the doorway into the living-room, I caught sight of my cousin's wife curled up on the couch, the warm rays of the autumn sun streaming down on her as she enjoyed a well-deserved sabbath 'rest'.

✛

What Moses meant

Although the following Friday had promised it, the early arrival of winter on the prairies still came as a bit of a shock to the system, even for someone like me who'd grown up with it. For Hilda, whose Irish upbringing left her singularly unprepared for such events, awaking to a thick blanket of snow in the middle of October was even more traumatic. Thankfully, somewhere down in the bowels of the house, I knew that our ancient furnace was doing its best to keep the temperature inside at least marginally higher than it was outside. As I huddled under the blankets, I thought of Exodus and the prohibition on lighting fires on the sabbath (35:3). I knew that Jerusalem wasn't as cold as Moose Jaw, but somehow felt that the orthodox Jews there would be as appreciative of their furnace pilot light as I was of mine. Of course, whatever our house lacked in terms of heat was more than compensated by the warmth we had come to expect from our little church down the road. It was, no doubt, the promise of this warmth, and perhaps also the sound of the baby stirring, that encouraged us to emerge from beneath the covers and brave the elements.

I didn't always look forward to the sermons our pastor preached, but I was particularly interested in what he would have to say about today's passage. Without either the blessing or the burden of a lectionary to constrain them, pastors in my church tradition are at liberty to preach from whichever passage seems most appropriate. The problem with this approach is that, for many pastors, some passages (like, for instance, the bulk of those found in Leviticus) don't seem appropriate to much at all and are thus never preached. At the same time, there are other texts that have drawn preachers of all sorts in almost every era—passages like the Ten Commandments. In a moment of inspiration, insanity or perverse irony, our pastor had decided to entitle his series on the decalogue 'The ten best ways to wreck your life'.

After an obligatory opening joke, he announced his intention to take us on a 20-minute tour of what the Bible says about the sabbath. Now, the Bible says a fair amount about the sabbath and certainly far more than anyone can say in 20 minutes, but in our church, as in many, the most important commandment is the eleventh: 'Thou shalt not be late for lunch.' In order to keep this particular commandment, the pastor couldn't afford to linger too long at the fourth one, which everyone knew was 'Thou shalt keep the sabbath'. Perhaps sensing congregational sloth, he spent nearly as much time reminding us about the six days we should be working as the one day we shouldn't. He also reminded us that when Moses said 'sabbath', what he really meant was Sunday. Of course, a church like ours hardly needed reminding of this. After all, what else could Moses have meant? Everyone knew that Sunday was the sabbath. It had been for as long as anyone in our church could remember. What our pastor knew full well, but had no time to explain, was that when Moses said 'sabbath' he did not mean Sunday at all. He meant exactly what he said: the sabbath was the seventh day and the seventh day was Saturday. I knew that if our pastor had taken the time to explain this, burnt roast dinners would probably have been the least of his worries. The local Seventh Day Adventist church was less than five minutes' walk from ours and thus, both geographically and theologically, too close for comfort.

If there had been more Jews in Moose Jaw, our church might have been more aware of the fact that they celebrated their sabbath the day before ours. Certainly, many of the first Christians were well aware of it, because many of them were as Jewish as Jesus himself had been. For these early Jewish Christians, the Sunday celebration of Jesus' resurrection didn't replace the Saturday sabbath. It took its place alongside it, so that the Jews who believed in Jesus could remain connected with their community.

Of course, many Christians who weren't Jews when they believed in Jesus (and even some who were) were more than a little wary of this early experiment with the two-day weekend. After all, wasn't the whole point that the salvation of Jesus' followers didn't depend on keeping the law of the sabbath? That certainly seemed to be the point Paul was trying to make when he wrote to the early church, and, in the centuries that followed, the Christians who weren't Jewish seemed to take the point seriously. Christians like Ptolemaeus and Tertullian became convinced that the commandment to keep the sabbath shouldn't be kept literally by resting, like the Jews did, but instead should be kept spiritually by devoting not one day but every day to God. Others, however, like Eusebius and perhaps Origen, believed that the sabbath should indeed be kept literally, but not on Saturday. Instead, it should be kept on Sunday, when Christians had already been resting from their work for at least part of the day to meet together for worship. By the time the Emperor Constantine declared 'the day of the Sun' to be an official day of rest on 3 March 321, some Christians were already treating it a lot like the sabbath anyway, though not always by resting for the whole of it.

Nevertheless, ever since that time, there have been Christians who have understood the fourth commandment to keep the sabbath not so much as God's will as simply a good idea, and one that has made it easier to worship their God. On the other hand, there have always been those for whom the fourth commandment is not merely a good idea but God's will, first for the people of Israel and eventually for his people in all times and in all places. For most of these Christians, the question remains: if the Israelite sabbath always fell on a Saturday, how could Moses have meant for the sabbath to be celebrated by Christians on Sunday? On our way home this Sunday, the stillness and silence of the Adventist church one block to the north reminded me that, for some Christians, the answer to this question was simple: he didn't.

✢

The bounty of heaven

Before the morning service at our church, a young woman carrying a baby about the same age as ours sat down in the adult Sunday school class. Our pastor had recently encouraged us to look out for newcomers and welcome them to the church, so I did. I was sure I'd never seen her before but she seemed more at ease than most first-time visitors I'd encountered in my time at the church. I wondered if this wasn't, in fact, her first time but perhaps her second or third. So, to be on the safe side, I asked, 'How long have you been coming to our church?' She smiled warmly. 'Oh, about two or three…' I was so sure she was going to say 'weeks' that I almost said it for her—but she didn't. She said '… years'. The scale of my miscalculation and the embarrassment that would have resulted had I finished her sentence left me speechless for a moment. That moment's hesitation was more than enough for her to notice and feel the need to offer an explanation. She had, she said, been going to one of the other services for most of that time, and while Hilda and I had been away over the summer, she had begun coming to the one we attended.

The woman seemed to be on her own with the baby and, again without thinking, I asked if her husband was also at church. While several potentially awkward answers to this question flashed through my mind, hers, when it came, was anything but. He was neither dead nor delinquent. He was a farmer. Like a few of the other farmers in the area, he still had crops in the field instead of in the barns where they belonged. Whether he was usually in church or not, I had no way of telling, but the reason he wasn't there this morning was that after several dank and dreary days, Constantine's 'day of the Sun' had dawned bright, dry and ideal for harvesting. The Holy Roman Emperor himself would have understood. While his edict had made the Sunday officially restful for city folks, it also made it clear that 'in the country... persons engaged in agriculture may freely and lawfully continue their pursuits; because it often happens that another day is not so suitable for grain-sowing or for vine-planting; lest by neglecting the proper moment for such operations the bounty of heaven should be lost.'[1]

Later that day, as I drove out to the college where I taught during the week, the stubble in the fields suggested that whatever bounty heaven had seen fit to bestow on our farmers was almost all collected. The nearer I got to the little town where the college sat, the less I looked forward to getting there. In this case, 'there' wasn't the college itself but the President's house, and the occasion was a reception for student leaders that I'd been invited to as Dean. I wasn't in the habit of resenting receptions. In fact, I usually quite liked them. Nor was it the students, the faculty or even the President that prompted the protest I felt rising up within me as I drove. As I reached the exit for the town, it struck me that the problem was that I was here on a Sunday. Although I was driving past the darkened windows of the college, the nagging sensation was that I was returning to work. Indeed, for many, a reception filled with people they don't know and conversations they don't want isn't just work, it's hard work—and, for a few, it's work of the very worst kind. In my case, it was enough like work to remind me that even in the short time I had been seeking the sabbath, I had come to value it more than I'd imagined.

My rediscovery of sabbath seemed to be taking place at a time when the town and community that the college called home was deciding that the sabbath wasn't quite as sacred as it once had been. There was much that was healthy in this, particularly given that, for decades, many had been convinced that keeping the sabbath was essential for their salvation. In this Christian college town, not so many years before, the sabbath had been a day of strict rules and stringent regulations, a day where the rhythm of morning service, afternoon rest and evening service was as regular as the rising of the sun at dawn and its setting at day's end. It was a day where the silence was broken not by the sound of lawn-mowers but only by the songs of the congregation spilling out of the chapel before noon and again at night. It was a day when ties were optional only for those students who didn't mind suffering the consequences of extra work duty when they were caught without one. Not unlike the ancient group that preserved the Dead Sea Scrolls in the dust of the Judean desert, this prairie community's isolation allowed it to protect not only the sabbath itself but also its own ideas about what should and shouldn't be done on it. Indeed, supported by the farmers whose fields fed them, and insulated from the erosion of the sabbath in the world outside, the college and its community kept the sabbath longer and better than most—so long and so well, perhaps, that when the 'rest' eventually began to be relaxed several years ago, the loss was lauded by some but lamented by many others.

For the family farmers still left in the area, the sabbath rest remains one of the hallmarks of the old ways and olden days. For them, the words of the Puritans ring as true at the beginning of the 21st century as they did when they were written at the end of the 16th: 'Though the corn be in danger, yet better were [it] for us, that it should rot on the ground than for us by... breach of the Sabbath, to treasure up unto our selves wrath against the day of wrath.'[2]

✛

31 October

Hallowing the past

In the church I grew up in, the weekly worship service became, over the course of several years, an event for adults only. It wasn't that there was anything shady going on, just that whatever good things were going on were pretty obviously not geared for children. One reason was that, in various rooms around the church, much was being done expressly for children, but this wasn't the only reason or even perhaps the most important one. At some point, it had been decided that a Sunday morning service for seekers was really no place for kids.

In the church I was now a grown-up in, there seemed to be just as much going on for children but the weekly worship service was, for the first quarter of an hour at least, very much for the whole family. Every week without fail, some brave soul would make their way to the front of the church and announce, sometimes with thinly disguised fear in their voice, that it was time for 'Children's Moments'. Moments (and usually only a few of them) was all it took for everyone under the age of seven to pour from the pews and stomp, stumble and generally stampede up the aisles in the direction of the platform.

On this day, the children were offered the opportunity to take an imaginary oar and row the boat along with the disciples as the story of 'Jesus walking on the water' was told in great detail. Finally, after rather more rowing than most of the children were used to, the storyteller's voice filled with the fear that the disciples themselves surely felt when they mistook Jesus for a ghost.

Although the children didn't bat an eyelash at what the Gospels take to be a garden-variety ghost, when our pastor regained the pulpit he felt obliged to excuse the mention of anything other than the Holy Ghost on a Sunday—even if this Sunday did happen to be Hallowe'en. The fact that today was Hallowe'en was not news to our congregation's school-age children, but, perhaps not surprisingly, it had escaped my attention.

When I was a child, I had been taken trick-or-treating by my mother, if only to justify the long hours spent transforming me into anything from the gingerbread man to Spiderman. At the same time, we children were always steered well clear of what my mother saw as the darker side of the day. Her task was made much easier by the fact that neither she nor any of us then knew that the origins of Hallowe'en lay in the pagan religions of the Celts and Romans. In Celtic religion, 31 October was celebrated as Samhain, the day when the souls of the dead returned to earth to cause trouble. As late as the eighth century, people were finding it so hard to forget the Samhain festivities that Pope Boniface did his best to trump them by declaring the next day, 1 November, to be All Saints' or All Hallows' Day, a day for celebrating Christian saints and martyrs. But old habits die hard and eventually the new day and All Hallows' Eve became again an occasion for dressing up as saints, angels and devils and honouring the dead. Only in the 19th century did Hallowe'en begin to become what it is, by and large, today: an evening of costumes and sweets, sponsored (in North America, at least) by the companies who sell them.

As we walked down our avenue that afternoon, after hearing the story of the disciples on the lake, I noticed that the houses decorated for Hallowe'en sported good-natured ghosts and witches doing their best not to look too wicked. In fact, on the whole, these houses seemed decidedly less scary than some of the ones whose skeletons were not allowed out of the closet. Whether the houses were decorated or not, I doubted that the inhabitants cared or were even aware that trick-or-treating today recalls both the ancient pagan idea of leaving food outside houses to appease the spirits and the tradition with which the Church tried to replace it—the handing out of 'soul cakes' in exchange for a promise to pray for the dead. With Hallowe'en, as with much at the beginning of the 21st century, it seems, the sacred is giving way to the secular.

So too with Sunday. The day has become our sabbath, but its very name betrays its mixed pedigree and gradual evolution from ancient times. The fact that the Day of the Sun was already venerable when it was officially declared a day of rest by Constantine suggests that it wasn't just the Son who was being worshipped on the first day of the week, but also the sun. Revered by ancient Israel's neighbours to the east as Shamash, and by those in Egypt to the south as Ra, the sun was also a favourite of the Romans, who decided to honour the God they called Solis with a day of his own. Just as the Jewish seventh day was being superseded by the Christian Lord's day on the first of the week, so too was the Roman seventh day, Saturn's day, being eclipsed by the day of the Sun. While there were numerous advantages in adopting Sunday as the Christian sabbath, it was also potentially confusing, which is why one of the early Church Fathers, Tertullian, wanted to make it perfectly clear that even though Christ was indeed the light of the world, Christians most certainly did not worship the sun. Eventually, Tertullian's point was beside the point, not only because fewer and fewer people continued to worship the sun but also because worship of the Son and the keeping of his sabbath received the sanction of the state.

While the days of Christendom have long since past and many Christians today seem to be turning their backs on the sabbath, the countries in which many of them live continue to observe a sabbath of sorts by keeping closed a whole host of government agencies including, for instance, the post office. The irony, seldom appreciated by Christians today, is that even though the sabbath has been almost entirely secularized in the West, if you work for the government the venerable Day of the Sun is still seen very much as sacred.

✝

Worshipping with the Warriors

As Saturday afternoon wound down and my mind turned to the sabbath once more, I began to wonder whether the town in which I lived wasn't a bit more religious than it seemed. It occurred to me that all across our little community, people were already beginning to look forward with anticipation to the coming evening. I knew that a bit later on, several thousand of them would be gathering in the largest building in town to sing, laugh and perhaps even cry together as everyone from lawyers to bricklayers put aside their worldly worries and turned their attention to higher things. For some, of course, it would be little more than an empty ritual, the kind of thing to attend this week for no other reason than that they had attended the previous one. But for others, what they would see and hear this evening would be the undeniable highlight of their week—a near-mystical experience to be relived and related to family and friends. When it came right down to it, our town loved ice-hockey.

The fact that I would be joining the 'congregation' on this night had less to do with a long-lost love for ice-hockey than with a promise Hilda and I had made to a friend. We had met Randy through our church's community ministry several years earlier and soon discovered that once you had met Randy, it was hard to forget him, for two reasons. One was that Randy suffered from a mental illness which made it difficult for him to do anything very quickly. It wasn't that he didn't have a lot on his mind. The problem was that when he got excited or nervous, he found it difficult to get what was on his mind out of his mouth, and what did come out wasn't always easy to understand either. The second thing that was immediately apparent on meeting Randy was that he liked sports a lot and ice-hockey most of all. So when Randy called one afternoon to invite Hilda and me along with him to watch the Warriors, we phoned the babysitter and went to buy our tickets. Watching hockey was certainly not how we'd imagined beginning our sabbath, but as we thought more about it, we realized that that wasn't really the point. The point was that it was Randy's idea and that he wanted nothing more than to share this experience with us.

The arena was nearly full—a testimony to the town's devotion to their local team. Not only had a third of the season now passed without the Warriors registering a single victory, but their most recent loss had come the previous night at the hands of tonight's opponents. Expecting the worst, we settled into our seats for what seemed certain to be a long night but, after trading goals near the beginning of the game, the hometown heroes scored twice to take a two-goal lead. Much to our surprise, Hilda and I found ourselves caught up in the enthusiasm of the crowd as we con-templated the prospect of the Warriors' first victory of the season. Again, to our surprise—though not, I suspect, to the surprise of more faithful fans—the visiting team saw impending defeat as an excuse to turn the hockey game into a free-for-all, as teams in this particular league were known to do. As the ice became littered with discarded hockey equipment and the Warriors took it upon themselves to live up to their name, the arena was instantly trans-formed. The crowd, which had been well-mannered throughout, was turned into a screaming, rabid mob by the impromptu brawl that had broken out on the ice below.

The fact that the scene in this arena was not much different from what went on in an ancient Roman one didn't seem to be bothering anyone. Nor should it have surprised us. Sports of all sorts have been around since well before the Romans, and are often played on days of rest and recreation like the sabbath. As

I watched the combatants being separated and the sticks they'd strewn across the ice being collected, I wondered whether the officials should perhaps have read the 17th-century *Book of Sports* before lacing on their skates. In it, King James I made it clear that on the sabbath 'no offensive weapons were to be carried or used during the time of recreation'. The fact that James also barred 'the meaner sort of people' from bowling tells us how different our century is from his. So does his decision to rule out the baiting of bears or bulls on Sunday, but to allow it the rest of the week. While I find it hard to agree with the Puritans that no sports of any kind belong on Sunday, I can see why many since have thought that some sports belong less on the Lord's day than others.

When play eventually resumed, the Warriors must have wished it hadn't. Having lost the battle, they promptly proceeded to lose the war, conceding a couple of goals in rapid succession before capitulating entirely in the final stages. As the game reached its conclusion, the home team's frustration boiled over and, to the excitement of the remaining fans, a repeat of the earlier mayhem ensued. As we left our seats and made our way through the disgruntled remnants of the crowd toward the exit, I found myself wondering whether tonight had been a part of my seeking of sabbath or whether we would have been wiser to have given the Warriors a wide berth. As the three of us walked toward the car park, I came to the conclusion that although I wouldn't soon return to the arena on my sabbath evening, the chance for me to spend a couple of hours in the company of a friend was enough to redeem the time.

✣

Around the table

I couldn't figure out why I found myself feeling festive on Saturday evening, until Hilda asked me to check the chicken. Only then did I realize that the warm, well-seasoned smell of roast chicken which had been wafting through the house all evening had convinced my nose that Christmas had come early or that Thanksgiving had come again. In our house, the only time the roasting pot emerged from the cupboard was on special occasions, but when I was growing up in my parents' house the presence of the pot on the stove was a marker of the sabbath. So committed was my mother both to her roast and to having it ready on our return from the morning service that she would often rise early on a Sunday morning in order to season the roast *du jour* before depositing it in the oven. Long experience of feeding five hungry mouths—the hungriest of which often belonged to her husband—had convinced her that if roast meat wasn't on the table soon after our return from church, the combination of empty stomachs and pent-up energy would soon turn an idyllic Sunday dinner into a disaster. Such a disaster could be averted, my mother had learned, through the use of that miracle of modern technology, the oven timer—a feature that she must have seen as sent straight from heaven. But one day, an incident took place that became so famous, indeed infamous, in our family that it was henceforth and thereafter referred to only as 'The Roast' and rarely at all when my mother was in the room.

As is often the case with disastrous accidents, a failure of technology was not to blame, but simple human error. After countless years of getting us home in time to retrieve beautiful, well-cooked roasts from the oven, it was perhaps inevitable (and, of course, entirely forgivable) that my mother should miscalculate eventually. It is safe to say that no one will ever know when the beef she placed in the oven that Sunday morning was ready to come out. Perhaps it was about the time the preacher reached his third point. I, for one, suspect that it may have been done before he even reached the pulpit. What we do know is that the roast was done well before any of us got home, and that by the time we did get home it was well past well done. It was so far past well done that we could see the disaster through the windows—the smoky haze hanging in the air like a pall—before we could smell it. While the smell of roasting chicken lives long in the memory, it cannot compare with the indelible imprint left on my olfactory nerve by the smell of burnt beef that day—and the problem was that my nerve wasn't the only thing indelibly imprinted with it. Carpets, curtains, clothes, linen and even our wallpaper had to be either professionally cleaned or disposed of, so powerful was the smell that had penetrated every nook and cranny of our house. When we returned home after a few days in a hotel, the odour had dissipated considerably but by no means entirely, and five years later it could still be detected when the cupboard containing our plates was opened a bit too quickly.

As it happened, the only people deprived of Sunday dinner that fateful day were our family—a blessing made all the more unlikely by the fact that our table was often more crowded at lunch on Sunday than it was the rest of the week. Like many from their church, my parents went out of their way to open their home and make space at their dining-room table for guests on many a Sunday. Whether the visitor was a new face at church or a familiar friend of the family, they were invited to join us not just for dinner itself but for dessert and perhaps much of the afternoon as well. It was done less out of a sense of duty than simple Christian hospitality, or so it seemed to me.

Now that I had a family of my own and a dinner table with as much room as my parents', we didn't extend sabbath hospitality out of a sense of duty either—in fact, I realized, we didn't really extend it at all. It occurred to me that here was one more casualty of the loss of sabbath. By not protecting the sabbath, I was depriving myself not only of a much-needed day of rest, but also an opportunity to extend hospitality to others. Luke tells us in his Gospel (14:1) that, whatever their motives, even the Pharisees invited Jesus to join them for a sabbath meal, and it didn't seem clear to me why I should be doing any less. That was why Hilda and I decided to make a change by making extra space at our dinner table, not perhaps every Sunday but more often than we had been doing.

The next day, we shared our chicken with two couples who attended our church—one with a baby about the age of ours and the other with one on the way. Dinner was nothing grand, nor was it particularly gourmet. In the end, in fact, it was less work than we thought it would be because one couple appeared at the door with a salad and the other with a loaf of fresh bread that they'd picked up on the way. As we sat down to dinner and shared the bread along with the rest of the food, I was reminded that Luke also tells us of the Sunday when the resurrected Christ appeared to his disciples (24:13–35). We remember that it was by breaking the bread, blessing it and giving it to them that Jesus first made himself known to his friends on the Emmaus road, but I sometimes forget that as the shadows grew long on the road in front of them, it was they who took the first step of inviting him in that Sunday, not only to stay but to break bread as well.

✝

A society without a sabbath

Each year about this time, all across America and around the world, professors of the Bible ready themselves for a peculiar pilgrimage. Lectures are written and sometimes hastily rewritten, unfashionable tweed jackets are packed, and well-bound Bibles are stowed away for the journey. It is a pilgrimage that begins wherever each of us finds ourselves teaching, but a journey whose destination is different each year. Not every city is willing or able to play host to the thousands of pilgrims who descend when the Society of Biblical Literature announces its arrival. This year we were bringing our Bibles to Texas, not because the Lone Star state was running short of them but because, as winter laid hold of the continent, San Antonio seemed a more promising prospect than Cincinnati.

For those of us from north of the border, in Canada, the challenge was getting there. When you live in Moose Jaw, Saskatchewan, it's sometimes a bit of a challenge getting a flight to anywhere, but to get to San Antonio required three. The first brought me to Minneapolis, the second eventually to Memphis, and the further south my migration carried me, the more of my fellow pilgrims I met. On the last leg of my journey, there were so many of us that I wondered whether our books weighed more than our baggage. In the seat to my left sat a professor so thoroughly engrossed in a volume about ancient Israel that not even the flight attendant dared to disrupt the sacred history. Fortunately for me, the Jesuit priest on my right seemed as uninterested in his book as I was in mine, so the time passed quickly as the congeniality of the conversation carried us west from Tennessee and south toward Texas. It was hardly surprising that as we collected our baggage in San Antonio, and others did the same, the conversations around the conveyor belts suggested that the arrivals hall had become little more than an oversized faculty lounge.

Not surprisingly, much has changed since the Society's first meeting back in 1880. More people, more lectures, more denominations, more religions and, of course, much much more to do. With papers to hear, books to buy, jobs to find, receptions to attend and people to meet, the Annual Meeting has become the busiest weekend of the year for professional students of the Bible. But it wasn't always that way. The first meeting, in New York, was on a Friday. Nine years later, the meeting overflowed from Friday and began on Thursday, and after the Depression two days became three. Today, even three days isn't enough, and the meeting now spills on to a fourth.

The need for everyone to return home to teach means that, ironically enough, for the venerable Society of Biblical Literature, no day is sacred and certainly not Sunday. Nor is the Society's Sunday very restful—unless, of course, you find the din of booksellers flogging the latest theological bestseller soothing and the *ad nauseam* academic discussion of manuscripts relaxing. I realized this year, for the first time in all my years of attending, that I didn't. I realized that although I did find the academic buzz interesting and sometimes even quite stimulating, it was anything but relaxing. As I walked on Sunday morning through the conference centre and the press of the crowds, I could feel my search for sabbath being sabotaged by my own desire to hear everything, meet everyone and be everywhere. The feeling grew stronger and stronger as I walked, until I was suddenly overwhelmed by a desire to escape. But where?

Although my hotel was called The Riverwalk, I'd been too busy to appreciate that San Antonio might in fact have a river and that I might actually be able to walk along it. Moments later, I found some steps that led me down to the water's edge, and as I began to walk along it amid the roses and jasmine, I felt the river washing away much of the busyness of the last few days as it flowed past me. I continued for several minutes, meeting others from time to time, until over the palm trees I caught sight of the spire of a church on the street above. Unable to resist the urge to investigate, I climbed the steps from the river and walked on until eventually I stood before a modest Gothic church. Entering and finding only a few others there, I sat for a moment and then knelt to pray. After the incessant sound of voices, both my own and others' all weekend, the silence in that little church seemed to speak of sabbath.

As the time for worship drew nearer, the church began to fill slowly but steadily with folks from San Antonio's Eastside, but the locals were not alone. Among those who looked like tourists, I noticed one woman carrying a bag that bore the markings of the Annual Meeting. Reaching the end of the pew, she genuflected, crossed herself, entered the pew and knelt to pray. Then I noticed another, and then another. By the time the service began, several of my colleagues were scattered among the local congregation. In the middle of the unrelenting schedule of our conference, it was somehow reassuring to realize that I was not the only one who was seeking sabbath. I wondered if they felt what I felt—if they too were reflecting on the blessing that we had been given. While several thousand of our colleagues were heatedly debating the meaning of God's word, our sabbath had afforded us the opportunity to read and to hear it among God's people. As the reader came to the end of his Bible passage and declared it to be the word of the Lord, I wondered if anyone else's 'Thanks be to God' was like mine—not only a thankfulness for scripture, but also for the unexpected sense of sabbath I had found in San Antonio.

✝

The eighth day

For the Americans who had made the pilgrimage to Texas, the following week was a time for thanksgiving. Many were thankful to be returning home, even if it took those of us north of the border a bit longer to get there. Some were undoubtedly thankful to have survived yet another Annual Meeting without calamity, academic or otherwise. But for the majority of those who had met—those from the United States—it was a time for thanksgiving for the very good reason that the Annual Meeting in November was always followed by Thanksgiving. While Canadian turkeys meet their untimely end in October, the American celebration of Thanksgiving in November affords their southern cousins a slightly longer lease of life.

Although the American turkey may not have much to be thankful for at this time of year, the same can't be said for the American retailer. With Christmas on the horizon, the Friday following Thanksgiving has become one of the biggest shopping days of the year. Perhaps it is fitting that the nation readies itself to give gifts even as it is in the midst of giving thanks. But it is rather ironic that the season of Advent begins in the wake of shopping, football and feasting, particularly given that the Advent season was originally one of penitence and fasting.

For those who keep to a Christian calendar, the first Sunday of Advent marks the end of Ordinary Time—a time that is 'ordinary' not because it is banal or mundane (though it may be) but because it is a time to be ordered and counted. Although we pass Ordinary Time by counting up from the first week after Pentecost (Trinity

Sunday, Trinity 2, Trinity 3, and so on), it is, in a very real sense, a counting down—from the end of the Easter period to the advent of the nativity. While the secular world must wait until January for the turning of its year, for those within the faith the first Sunday of Advent is the first Sunday of the new year. In the sense that we count each Sunday as it passes, the time of Advent is no less 'ordinary' than the rest. In the sense that we are both counting up and counting down to Christmas, however, Advent is an extra-ordinary time in many ways.

For many of us, it is a time of extraordinary busyness—a time for concerts, plays and parties, even for those who don't otherwise indulge in such things. It's a time of unusual purchases and un-manageable credit cards, a time of extra essays and expectant stu-dents and far too little time to devote to either, as the academic term hurtles toward its conclusion. Advent is perhaps, above all and for all kinds of reasons, a time of extraordinary anticipation, a time of looking forward. For those beyond the faith, it is a time of looking forward to food and fellowship and family. For those within the faith, Advent is often a time of looking forward to looking back. It is an anticipation of a moment (and, in our frantic lives lived at frenetic pace, it is often little more than a moment) to look back at the coming of the Christ.

This is how I remember Advent as a child: my three sisters and I taking our turn (and, if we could, someone else's too) at the Advent calendar, as day by day, door by door, we counted down to the only day that really mattered to us. The final door, always larger and grander than the rest and the subject of keen competition, was forgotten when Christmas Day itself arrived: we had much more interesting things to open. But in the midst of the usual trappings and wrappings of Christmas, there were always reminders to look back. There was the the high drama and inevitable disaster of the Sunday school Christmas play—so exciting for us as children and by turns embarrassing and endearing for our parents. There was the Nativity set—stable and figurines—carefully unpacked and positioned appropriately. And of course, there was the family reading of the Nativity acount itself from the second chapter of Luke (always Luke) as we gathered round the hearth on Christmas Eve.

Only later did I discover that there was more to Advent than the manger—that for the church in the West, Advent has long been not only an anticipation of looking back to the first coming of Christ, but also an opportunity to look forward to his return. And on the first sabbath of Advent, the Gospel reading—the reading I turned to on this particular sabbath evening—was not from near the beginning of Luke but considerably closer to its end.

There will be signs in the sun, the moon, and the stars, and on the earth distress among nations confused by the roaring of the sea and the waves. People will faint from fear and foreboding of what is coming upon the world, for the powers of the heavens will be shaken. Then they will see 'the Son of Man coming in a cloud' with power and great glory. Now when these things begin to take place, stand up and raise your heads, because your redemption is drawing near. (Luke 21:25–28)

As I sat at the kitchen table with only my Bible for company, it occurred to me that while Christ's first coming is, for me, a fact of faith, thinking about his second coming represents in some sense a greater act of faith. I find it easier to celebrate that Christ came to earth long ago than to contemplate that Christ may come again at any moment. It's more comfortable and also comforting to reflect on historical certainty than eschatological possibility. Yet we are called to do so, and not just on Advent's first Sunday. As early as the second century, the Church Fathers began to see the end-time significance of the Lord's day: 'It is not the present Sabbaths that are acceptable to me, but the one that I have made, on which having brought everything to a rest, I will make the beginning of an eighth day, that is, the beginning of another world.'[3]

Although Sunday was the first day of the week, the fact that it followed on the heels of the seventh may have been what prompted early Christians to think of Sunday as the eighth day.

Maybe, also, the resurrected Christ's reappearance to his disciples 'eight days later' in the Gospel of John (20:26, RSV) had something to do with it. Or perhaps the lack of an 'evening and morning' to the seventh day in Genesis 1 suggested that the earthly sabbath rest gave way to a heavenly rest anticipated by Sunday, the eighth day. Wherever it came from, 'the eighth day' seems to have become a favourite way of referring to Sunday for the Fathers, including Gregory the Great, who saw the eighth day as symbolizing 'the bodily resurrection from death and the rejoicing at the glorious reunification of the soul with the flesh... the eighth day opens to us the vastness of eternity, through the light which follows after the seventh day'.[4]

The following morning, as I sat in church, the preacher happened to speak of the need for rest this Advent season, perhaps because he himself was in need of some. More important for me was the moment when a family from the church approached the candelabra at the front to light the first candle of Advent, the first rite of the coming season which had always caused me to look forward to looking back. I watched as the flame caught the wick, growing brighter and stronger as it took hold. Even from where I was sitting, near the back, this solitary point of light seemed to burn with unusual intensity. In its peculiar light, I found myself, for the first time at Advent, looking forward not only to the celebration of Christ's first day but also to the anticipation of his eighth day and the extraordinary rest promised by his eventual return.

✜

To do or not to do

Compared with many (perhaps most) ways of making a living, working in a theological college is by no means a hard lot. At some points, it is such a pleasure and a blessing that it hardly seems like work at all. But after a particularly heavy week of teaching and a house full of family and friends down to celebrate our daughter's first birthday, I was relishing the prospect of a restful sabbath. The only question I faced as the evening stretched out in front of me was 'With what kind of rest will I fill it?' My brother-in-law suggested a movie but, as I began to think about which one I'd like to see, my twin sisters announced that later that evening they were taking Hilda off to the cinema for a girls' night out. Since the arrival of our baby, opportunities for her to get out of the house had been rather few and far between, so it seemed obvious that I should stay in and she would go.

With a wife and child of his own, my brother-in-law was more than understanding and offered to rent a film and bring it over when our wives went out. Until then, however, the evening was mine, so I settled down on to the sofa and flicked on the television. Thanks to the satellite dish perched near the peak of our roof, I had instant access to countless channels promising unending entertainment—at least, in theory. In practice, I discovered that on this evening, as on so many others, the quantity of channels seemed to be inversely proportional to the quality of what they were showing. The more channels I checked, the less I wanted to watch, until eventually I switched off the television in frustration.

Perhaps this was no bad thing, I thought. Hilda and I had spent very little time together in the last several days and, with the baby upstairs asleep, now was our chance to enjoy some 'quality time' before my sisters arrived to whisk her away. When I found Hilda in the living-room, though, she was sitting in the midst of a pile of home-made and, for the most part, unmade Christmas cards. In recent days, her production had slowed and I could see that the 'factory' was now making up for lost time—running full-tilt in an attempt to make sure the cards reached their destinations by Christmas. With Hilda's attention focused squarely on the task at hand, it became clear after a few minutes that my attempts at meaningful conversation were less of a contribution to the process than a distraction from it. Not wanting to stand in the way of progress, I sat for a few minutes more on the couch and simply watched her work. But it wasn't long before I remembered that, like most workaholics, I'd much rather work myself than watch someone else do so.

I was still at a loss as to what to do with myself when the time came and then passed for Hilda to meet the twins at the cinema. As she rushed out of the door, which slammed with a thud, the house fell silent. I wandered around the house, consoling myself with the thought that my brother-in-law would soon call to announce that he was on his way over. When he did call, however, it was to announce that he was worn out, had an early start the next morning, and wouldn't be coming over after all.

Now, a sabbath evening that I had looked forward to full of anticipation suddenly seemed rather empty. Deprived of my visitor and without either the diversion of the baby or the distraction of the television, I felt my mind begin to wander down a well-worn path—a path that it typically wandered when it had nowhere else to go. I felt myself thinking about work—specifically, what work I might get done in the remainder of the evening. Why not? Given that there seemed to be nothing else to do, what harm could there be in it? Although I had no answers myself, the words of Isaiah, which I'd been teaching that week, echoed in my mind:

If you refrain from trampling the sabbath, from pursuing your own interests on my holy day; if you call the sabbath a delight and the holy day of the Lord honorable; if you honour it, not going your own ways, serving your own interests, or speaking idle words; then you shall take delight in the Lord. (Isaiah 58:13–14)

I knew that these words were written to Jews more than two and a half thousand years ago, but on this evening they spoke straight to my heart. Until then, my seeking of sabbath had been a search for personal space in the midst of a cluttered calendar and the worries of the world. In a sense, the sabbath I'd been seeking so far was an end in itself, not what it should have been and might yet be. Instead of being an end in itself, I realized that the sabbath I should have been seeking was really a means to an end far greater, an end we are called to aim for every day of our lives but perhaps especially on the sabbath—to take delight in our God. So, instead of sitting down to work, I sat down to pray. And as I did, in the stillness and silence of our front room, I felt a quiet contentment steal over my soul as, bit by bit, my mind turned away from my work and toward the one who works within us if only we will allow him.

Later, as I reflected on my strange evening, I was reminded of Richard Wurmbrand, the Romanian pastor who spent 14 years in a Communist prison for his faith, and three of those in solitary confinement. In the middle of the torture and isolation of those days, Wurmbrand recalled his experience of sabbath:

Things seem to be getting worse and worse. It is a Sabbath day. This time I am not only in a strait-jacket and gagged but I have heavy chains at my feet which prevent me from walking. A Sabbath day. The fullest Sabbath I have ever enjoyed in my life. I cannot disturb my rest even by a movement of my hands, feet or lips.[5]

While I still find it hard to explain why God allowed Wurmbrand to languish in prison for so long, his words helped me to understand in some small measure how an evening that allowed me no distractions, a sabbath evening that seemed so utterly empty, could eventually turn out to be one of the fullest of all.

+

Surviving Sunday school

With the arrival of our new pastor the previous summer, those
of us who had been shouldering the burden of the preaching were
suddenly freed up to explore other ways to contribute to the
church's ministry, so it was suggested that I move from preaching
the word to teaching it. The only slightly surprising thing about
this idea was that it hadn't been suggested before, given that
teaching the Bible is what I do for a living. And there, of course,
was the rub. In the mind of our Christian Education coordinator,
the reason I was best suited to the job was that it was my job. In
my mind, however, this was the very reason I was best advised to
steer clear of it altogether. It wasn't that I had anything against
teaching in the church—that would have been strange indeed for
the Dean of a theological college. In fact, the previous year I had
taught a midweek course to lay people at a church an hour down
the road from our town. No, the problem wasn't what or even
where I was being asked to teach; it was when. Like many traditional churches on th Canadian prairies, ours still offers people of
all ages the opportunity to attend 'Sunday school' before the
morning service. Unfortunately, part of my plan to reclaim some
kind of sabbath involved making sure that Sunday was the one day
when I wasn't at school.

The fact that I found myself hastily setting up my flipchart the
following Sunday in the improvised classroom in our church foyer
reflected both our coordinator's powers of persuasion and the fact
that part of me was quite easily persuaded. After all, I reminded

myself, since the time of Christ—and, in the case of the Jews, well before—there had always been room for the reading and teaching of scripture on the sabbath. In Luke 4:16–22, when Jesus stood up to read from Isaiah in the synagogue in Nazareth, it was what he said and how he said it that amazed his audience, not that he did it on the sabbath. If the ancient authorities may be believed, it wasn't just the Jewish synagogue that revolved around the scripture; so too did their schools, known in Hebrew as 'houses of the book'. Small wonder, then, that by the second century, Justin Martyr reports that Christians were also making space for both the reading of scripture and its explanation when they met on Sunday. Of course, it was only much later, in the 18th century, that churches in North America began to run Sunday schools and later still, in the following century, that these Sunday schools (and, in the case of synagogues, sabbath schools) became what they still are in many places today: a place and time for teaching the scriptures.

Since accepting the job, and for the better part of three months, I'd been doing my best with the adult Sunday school without being truly convinced that my best was proving good enough. Although my students at college were, of course, adults, the average age of my Sunday school class was easily twice mine, which explains why, after the first week, I was told to 'speak up'. After the second, I was reminded that the best way to finish on time is to start on time. And on the third, I was informed—though not in so many words— that the classes really were better before I'd taken over. For the sake of my predecessor, I certainly hoped they were.

Perhaps because my Sunday school class was neither studying for credit nor paying for the privilege, what little homework I assigned remained undone. This was less disruptive than it might have been, because the students seemed to be taking turns to attend in alternate weeks anyway. As we reached the middle of the term, I realized that my Sunday school teaching was beginning to feel a lot like work. In fact, it was beginning to feel more like work than what I did during the week at the college. I wondered whether anyone else at our church felt the same way as I did. After all, I was not the only person who taught all week at one school and then on Sunday at another. The basement was full of primary teachers wrestling with some of the same seven-year-olds they taught during the week. We weren't pastors, so why were we expected to give up our Sundays as if we were?

Such was my state of mind as I headed out of the door on this day and down toward the church, knowing that I would never have time to set up all the chairs and do the photocopying needed for this morning's class. When I arrived, however, I discovered, much to my surprise, that a couple of students had got there before me and set out the chairs of our ad hoc classroom on their own initiative. Although this unexpected blessing allowed me to start more or less on time, my heart sank when I discovered that only two of this week's group had been there the previous Sunday and that those two hadn't done their homework anyway. Not for the first time, I began to feel as if the term's theme, 'Making sense of suffering', was going to double as a fairly accurate description of my Sunday school class experience.

In the minutes that followed, however, something strange happened—something that I had little to do with, if only because after weeks of struggle I felt as if I had little to offer. As we began to read and talk about what Isaiah 24—27 might have to tell us about suffering, we soon found ourselves focusing on the words of Isaiah 26:19, 'Your dead shall live…'. I watched as these words began to be fulfilled in a strange and surprising way, as my class itself seemed to come to life. As we talked about Isaiah's picture of judgment day, God's destruction of the dragon, his calling of the elect, his punishment of the wicked and vindication of the righteous, the group became more animated than they had been all term. Maybe it was because they felt themselves to be nearer the end of their lives than I felt I was to mine. Or perhaps it was because, unlike my generation, who seem to be entranced by the here and now, their generation had always been more willing to anticipate the 'there and then' of the end times. Whatever it was, the idea that scripture anticipates the end of time as one solution to the suffering of the saints caught the imagination of my class in a way that few other ideas had. When we finally drew our conversation to a close, we were well past our usual stopping time, but no one seemed to notice.

As we prayed together before making our way into the main church along with the rest of the congregation, I thanked God for his word and the opportunity to come together as brothers and sisters and allow it to speak into our lives. Only later did I realize that, on this Sunday, I was perhaps most thankful for God's gracious reaffirmation that it was indeed possible to seek the sabbath even when you're teaching Sunday school.

+

The shortest sabbath

Since the arrival of the baby more than a year ago, I had found myself rising much earlier than I used to and often well before the sun. Of course, as autumn gave way to winter in our neck of the woods, even those without babies to wake them found themselves increasingly in the dark as the days grew shorter and the nights ever longer. In the dark, in more ways than one, was a bit how I felt as I sat down at my desk in the early morning to pull together my notes for this week's Sunday school. As the gloom gradually retreated, the light of my lamp seemed to weaken until finally the thin rays of the winter sun cut through the grey dawn of a new day—the shortest Sunday of the year.

According to the clock, of course, this particular Sunday was no shorter than any other, but with the winter solstice only days away, I knew that the light which had appeared late this morning would not linger long past five in the afternoon. My problem was that before the sun sank beneath the horizon, there was much to do— too much, if we wanted to be ready when the teaching staff from my faculty appeared for dessert and drinks later on that evening, as they'd been invited. Our plan had been to be ready well before Sunday morning, and we probably would have succeeded if it hadn't been for the previous 24 hours.

In addition to having the faculty round for dessert on Sunday evening, we had invited my car-pooling colleagues for dinner on Saturday night and agreed to coordinate the church's Christmas community lunch earlier that same afternoon. Only after we'd committed ourselves to all three events did we discover that all of them were happening within the space of 36 hours. When we realized our mistake, we did what we usually do in these situations: we panicked. Then, having panicked, we came up with a plan, which we hoped would keep us one step ahead. On Friday evening and Saturday morning, we would pitch in to prepare the Christmas meal at the church. As soon as it was over, we'd return home to make the lasagne and tidy up before my car-poolers and their partners showed up on our doorstep for dinner on Saturday evening. While cooking Saturday's dinner, the plan was to start preparing Sunday's desserts.

Armed with such a foolhardy plan, it's hardly surprising that we were behind almost before we began. By the time we got back from the church on Saturday afternoon, we barely had time to get ready for dinner later that evening, let alone think about desserts for the following one. And of course, by the time our dinner guests left us on Saturday evening, neither Hilda nor I were in any shape to be baking, if we wanted the results to be edible.

With a baby to feed, Sunday school to teach and a service to attend, the morning swept past me without so much as a pause. Before I knew it, we were home again and back in the kitchen. For those more practised in the culinary arts, whipping up several desserts in the space of a Sunday afternoon might have seemed a wonderful way to spend the sabbath. For me, it was the furthest thing from it. Between mincing dates and fretting over the flour, I managed to pass the entire afternoon preparing a single dessert of frankly dubious quality.

As I cleaned up, I recalled the mention of the sabbath in Exodus 16:23, where Moses reminds God's people, 'Tomorrow is a day of solemn rest, a holy sabbath to the Lord; bake what you will bake and boil what you will boil, and all that is left over lay by to be kept till the morning.' Here, in the very first reference to the sabbath by name in the Hebrew Bible, we see the radical nature of the rest God ordains. As necessary as it may seem, even the provision and preparation of our daily bread is but a distraction from the solemn rest of the holy sabbath, which it might otherwise erode. For the rabbis, this verse set forth the principle that whatever else the sabbath might have been for, it certainly was not for cooking. Small wonder, then, that the Gospels refer to the day of the sabbath eve as the day of preparation, for that's exactly what it was—a day of feverish anticipation and practical preparation of house and home for the holy sabbath to come. After all, as the rabbis knew full well, the one who takes 'trouble [to prepare] on the eve of the Sabbath can eat on the Sabbath, but he who has not troubled on the eve of the Sabbath, what shall he eat?'[6]

While we weren't quite ready to forsake cooking on the sabbath altogether, I saw for the first time the very real virtue of getting most of it done beforehand, like orthodox Jews still do today. If we had done so this weekend, my Sunday afternoon might have been spent not in the kitchen but curled up on the couch with a good book or out for a walk with my wife. In our eagerness to extend the hospitality of the sabbath, it was obvious to us both that we had overextended ourselves. In the midst of my sabbath seeking this weekend, I seemed to have ended up, inadvertently and un-intentionally, sabotaging it.

I stood at the window in our front room and watched as the sun dipped toward the horizon and the sky began to glow orange and hot as if it had suddenly been set alight. As the sun set and darkness descended, I realized that the reason I'd failed to find my sabbath this week was not because it was too short but because it was too full of the wrong things. While I regretted the rest that had been lost, as I returned to the kitchen and prepared for the arrival of our company I resolved to learn from my mistake and, in the weeks to come, resume my search for the sabbath.

St Stephen's

Being unexpectedly busy at college in the week leading up to Christmas, I found myself struggling even more than I usually did to get my shopping done before the 25th. A flurry of purchases at the local mall on the 23rd certainly helped, but as Christmas Day began to loom ever closer, I knew that my bid to find the perfect gift for Hilda was destined to fail miserably. And, to make matters worse, I wasn't the only one who knew.

Whether she had sensed my desperation or felt a hint of it herself as she had shopped for me, my wife—kind and generous woman that she is—offered me a way out. She offered to extend the deadline, just as I did from time to time for students in extenuating circumstances. Perhaps worried about what she might otherwise receive, Hilda suggested that instead of letting me try to find something in what little was left of the day before Christmas, we could go shopping together the day after Christmas. The fact that I was quickly running out of alternatives wasn't the only reason why her suggestion appealed. Her presence in the shop with me would, I was sure, spell the end of the agonizing indecision that had inevitably accompanied my solo expeditions. Gone would be the guesswork, as Hilda herself would sift through the bewildering multitude of colours, sizes and styles on sale and, almost certainly, on offer. And that was the last and perhaps best reason to take my wife up on her suggestion. After all, according to the flyers filling our mailbox and the commercials on television, on Boxing Day not only was everything *for* sale, everything was *in the* sale.

Having been raised in a family where thriftiness was next to godliness, I was a sucker for a sale, whether I actually needed what was on special offer or not. And I was not the only one. Happily ignoring the miracle of Boxing Day—that shelves picked clean the day before Christmas are carefully restocked for year-end clearance the day after—I had often joined the countless others across the country who celebrate Boxing Day the only way we know how: by visiting the big boxes in which our favourite retail outlets are found and leaving them with the slightly smaller boxes in which our favourite toys are sold. For the sake of both Hilda's belated Christmas gift and my limited budget, I had decided that I was willing to brave the madding crowds—and then I realized that, this year, Boxing Day was also a Sunday.

For companies wanting to make the most of the Boxing Day bonanza, the only difference this made was that the early-bird bargains were delayed from 8 in the morning until 10—the earliest they were allowed to open on a Sunday. The fact that several of them preferred to open illegally and pay a hefty fine for the privilege suggests that they were banking on the triumph of shopping over *shabbat*.

For Hilda and me, however, it was hard to imagine finding the sabbath we were seeking in the press of people and our own conspicuous consumption. Instead, we did what we usually did on a Sunday but only rarely on Boxing Day: we went to church. For a change, the church we went to was not our own. On this, the feast day of St Stephen, we decided that it was only fitting to visit one of the many churches named in his honour—in this case, St Stephen's Anglican, a small and unassuming church not far away. As is often the case in churches of its size, the fact that we were there for the first time was all the more obvious because so few others were in attendance, but the welcome within was as warm as the wind outside was cold.

Stephen was, according to Acts 6:5 and 8, a man full of faith, grace, power and the Spirit, and this seems evident when we consider the fate he was destined to suffer—the fate of his Saviour, who also proclaimed the gospel and paid the same deadly price. Like his Saviour, Stephen suffered as a servant not only of his God but also of his people. When we first hear of him, it is as one of the seven appointed by the apostles to make sure that no one in need among the believers in Jerusalem would be neglected (Acts 6:1–6). Perhaps that's part of the reason why, according to the Christmas carol, 'on the feast of Stephen' Good King Wenceslas encourages us:

> *Therefore, Christian men, be sure,*
> *Wealth or rank possessing,*
> *Ye who now will bless the poor*
> *Shall yourselves find blessing.*

How St Stephen's day ended up as Boxing Day in England and eventually elsewhere, no one knows for certain. Perhaps, the first boxes of Boxing Day were the ones given by nobles to their servants the day after Christmas. Or maybe they were originally those in which alms for the poor were collected up until Christmas, and out of which they were distributed the next day. It felt to me that either sort of box was far preferable to the kind on which I had often focused on Boxing Days gone by—boxes that had more to do with getting than with giving, boxes that seemed entirely out of place on the sabbath anyway, but especially on one when we remembered St Stephen.

Next year, I knew, Boxing Day would be different. I knew that it would fall on Monday rather than landing on a day of rest. But even as I knew this, I also hoped that this year's experience of the first sabbath after Christmas would leave a lasting impression. I hoped that next year, at this time, I would remember this year's meeting of St Stephen and the sabbath as not merely coincidental but, in fact, truly providential.

✢

A woman's work is never done

The passing from one year to the next is often a time for reflection, and with New Year's Day winding down and the sabbath eve approaching, I felt some small sense of satisfaction. Although my search for a day of rest over the past few months had been more challenging than I'd imagined it would be, I felt sure that Hilda and I were well on our way to recovering a sabbath in our lives. But in the midst of this satisfaction, I felt something else, something that prevented me from savouring it: I felt a sneaking suspicion that one of us was getting more rest than the other.

When you work in an office or a library or a faculty staffroom, the sabbath becomes—and had increasingly become for me—a sort of escape. It was a kind of work-free zone between the end of one long week and the beginning of another. But what if you don't work in an office? What if you work at home? Or, more to the point, what if your work is your 'home', as Hilda's had become since the arrival of our baby the previous year? I began to wonder whether 'we' really had recoved a sense of sabbath or whether the only one who had was 'me'.

Although Hilda had recently returned to work part-time, I knew (without really wanting to admit it) that since then, the only 'part-time' aspect of how much she worked was how much she was paid. After all, the fact that she was home less didn't mean that there was less at home to do. No longer a full-time homemaker, yet still intent on making our house a home, Hilda was slowly being squeezed between the sabbath we were seeking and the incessant demands of cleaning, cooking and caring for our daughter.

In doing our best to protect the sabbath, we had discovered early on what many others had discerned long ago: when you set aside one day, the day before sometimes becomes even busier. The jobs we might otherwise have done on Sunday, like going out for groceries or staying in to fix a leaky tap, now quickly filled each Saturday to overflowing. After several months of practice, I had learnt to leave whatever work was left over to another day, but I began to wonder about my wife. Our preparations for the sabbath were nothing compared to those of the rabbis, but I realized that the one characteristic I did share with them was a tendency to let Hilda take care of things—which is perhaps why the Talmud had to remind the sages to give their wives a hand before *shabbat*: 'Raba salted fish, Rabbi Huna lit the lamp. Rabbi Papa plaited the wicks, Rabbi Hisda cut up the beetroots. Rabbah and Rabbi Joseph chopped wood. Rabbi Zera kindled the fire.'[7]

Before the evening meal in the Orthodox tradition, it is still the woman's privilege to light the candles that welcome the holy day, but for the rabbis' wives and for mine, I began to see that the weekly arrival of 'Queen Sabbath' wasn't really as restful as I'd assumed. If food was needed, it was Hilda who served it, and when a nappy was dirty, it was Hilda who changed it. While I was doing my best to slow our life down on the sabbath, my wife was making sure that it didn't grind to a halt altogether. At some point on this sabbath evening, it dawned on me that the day of rest I had been recovering was starting to resemble the sabbath of my youth, when the rest of us rested and my mother kept right on going.

Disconcerted by my discovery, I resolved to give Hilda a real rest this sabbath—or at least as much of a rest as I could possibly give her. And so it was that on Sunday morning, with some fear and no little trepidation, I took over. As Hilda slept, I rose early to wrestle with my daughter's dirty nappy. Her breakfast proceeded by trial and error—trial because instead of cereal, bread or fruit, she wanted yoghurt, and error because yoghurt was the one thing I didn't have.

By the end of 'breakfast' in only the loosest sense of the word, I was ready to crawl back into bed. My sabbath morning was only an hour old and already I was exhausted. Happy to be released from her highchair, my daughter headed off to play the only way that she knew how: by toddling toward the stairs and screaming randomly and perhaps for no other reason than to hear the sound of her own excruciatingly loud voice. In the hours that followed, it became readily apparent that taking care of a toddler leaves little time for the kind of sabbath to which I'd become accustomed. Instead, I was forced to seize the sabbath where I could find it, during church when she was in the crèche, or after lunch when she went down for her nap.

Not long after Anna awoke from her nap, Hilda reminded me that it would soon be time for dinner. I was about to remind her that it was far too early for our dinner when I realized that she wasn't talking about our dinner at all, but our daughter's. Only after hers was finished (this time in the fullest sense of the word) could I turn my attention to ours. With Hilda engrossed in the newspaper and my daughter alternately tugging at my trousers and toppling over into a heap on the floor, the most I could muster was an omelette, which thankfully dirtied comparatively few dishes, given that I was the one who would be washing them.

By the time Anna was ready for bed, the sabbath was finished—and so was I. While my busyness hadn't allowed me much of a rest on this sabbath, it did remind me that it was often Hilda's busyness that had allowed me to rest on the previous ones. Perhaps that's why, after the wife lights the candles to inaugurate the sabbath and her husband offers the *brachot*, the blessings, he saves the best for last: 'An excellent wife who can find? She is far more precious than jewels. The heart of her husband trusts in her, and he will have no lack of gain. She does him good, and not harm, all the days of her life' (Proverbs 31:10–12).

✝

9 January

Vespers

Although the idea of Sunday as a day of rest took hold only later among Christians who weren't already Jews, the Lord's Day was from the very beginning a day of devotion. It is well known that the earliest followers were not only devoted to the Lord whose day it was; they were also committed to each other and the gathering of the saints for fellowship and worship. And so it has been ever since on the sabbath. The patterns have changed with the passing of time and the transforming of traditions, but the fact remains: Christians have been coming together on the sabbath for as long as anyone can remember, and certainly much longer than I can. For us as children, there were Bible classes at 9.45, a children's worship service at 11, and then running, running, running to find my parents through a foyer filled with giants—a forest of dark trousers and winter coats and smiling, familiar faces.

But while the virtues of 'morning church' were never in doubt for us as children, the same could not be said for its evening counterpart, which went by what always seemed to me the rather sinister sounding name of Vespers. Perfectly timed to deprive us of television's *Wonderful World of Disney*, the evening service offered children little by way of compensation until it was over, when the fun would finally begin. While the grown-ups filled the foyer for a second time, we disappeared to the sports hall until they showed up to drag us out and take us home. If we were lucky, church would be followed by 'fellowship hour'—an extremely exciting event that not only allowed us to extend whatever game we were playing but also furnished us with an exotic array of sandwiches and cakes to fuel our fun.

Most of the time, however, we weren't quite so lucky and, more often than not, as Sunday afternoon slipped past and the evening service drew ever nearer, we wished that Disney would triumph and that Vespers would somehow disappear. And the funny thing was, it did. Not immediately—in fact, almost imperceptibly—the evening service at our church began to fade away, until eventually Vespers vanished altogether, leaving Sunday's evening meal time to Snow White and the Seven Dwarves.

Our church wasn't the only one. As the 20th century wound down, the Sunday evening service—so long a fixture in many traditional congregations—seemed to wind down with it. I wondered whether its disappearance was simply a result of the sabbath's erosion or perhaps, in fact, one of the reasons for it. Now that I was seeking out the sabbath anew, I was in the strange position of feeling quite keenly the absence of a service that I had never enjoyed and whose loss I had never lamented. In its absence, my sabbath didn't so much end as simply peter out, as if the day of rest itself was somehow worn out or forced to relent before the demands of the working week to come. I wondered what it might be like to see the sabbath out on Sunday in much the same way that Jews welcomed the *shabbat* in on a Friday—with a service.

Reckoning that our church was unlikely to begin a Sunday evening service simply on our say-so, Hilda and I resolved to hold our own Vespers as our sabbath day gave way to evening. As a child, I had no idea and no reason to care that Vespers had been around for a long time before I or any other Methodist appeared on the scene: when St Benedict referred to the sixth hour of the divine office in his time, he was already calling it *vespera*, which was quite conveniently the Latin term for 'evening'. In the Roman church since, the service of Vespers has changed little more than the name: as Sunday afternoon gives way to evening, the sounds of psalms, hymns, canticles and prayer still ring out across the Catholic world.

Not surprisingly, our service was far simpler: reading and reflection, invocation and blessing. In the midst of it, the text that spoke most loudly to me was not from the Bible but from Thomas Merton:

Now the Fathers of the Church well understood the importance of a certain 'holy leisure'—otium sanctum. *We cannot give ourselves to spiritual things if we are always swept off our feet by a multitude of external activities. Busyness is not the supreme virtue, and sanctity is not measured by the amount of work we accomplish. Perfection is found in the purity of our love for God, and this pure love is a delicate plant that grows best where there is plenty of time for it to mature.* [8]

Hilda and I read and prayed together in our front room as the light was fading and our sabbath ending. Even as it ended, however, I felt as if it was, in a sense, only just beginning—just beginning to be more than simply the absence of work. It was becoming something like the leisure of which the Fathers spoke: not a hedonistic leisure, but one that was hallowed and set apart for a holy purpose. What this purpose was, and why it was holy, was fully impressed upon my heart only as we finished. Without a choir to sing the canticle or a cathedral in which to sing it, we chose to listen instead to the beautiful voice of a friend whose recording of the Nunc Dimittis we had kept. It was a song she had sung on a Sunday, a song that had been sung for centuries in the Orthodox tradition of the Vespers and was undoubtedly being heard in many of its churches even as the two of us sat listening in rapt silence:

Lord, now lettest thou thy servant depart in peace,
according to thy word:
For mine eyes have seen thy salvation,
Which thou hast prepared before the face of all people;
A light to lighten the Gentiles, and the glory of thy people Israel.
FROM LUKE 2:29–32

Having finally caught a glimpse of the only thing worth living for, Simeon speaks of God's ultimate purpose for both Jew and Gentile: the Christ who is, as the old man saw so clearly, 'thy salvation'. As the words settled on my soul, and the strains of Herbert Howell's setting died away, I began to understand that there could be no more perfect purpose, no holier leisure than to rest and reflect on the Lord whose sabbath it was then and still is today.

+

16 January

Come, my beloved

Even before I began to search again for a sabbath, I was never really likely to forget Sunday altogether—not while we continued to worship in a church like ours, which had met every Sunday for a century and was unlikely to stop doing so any time soon. The very regularity of the sabbath's appearance in our lives makes it a difficult day to forget, even if it is not always easy to observe. In much the same way, although I seldom note and even less frequently celebrate every signpost that dots our Christian calendar as we move from Advent through to Pentecost and Trinity each year, I find myself less likely than ever before to let these sacred days pass unobserved.

After several years of marriage, the same might be said for one other day on my calendar—a day whose sacredness is confirmed by the seriousness of failing to celebrate it, a day that can determine the fate of many days that follow, for better if it's remembered and certainly for worse if forgotten. Just ask any husband who's missed their wife's birthday!

This year, perhaps providentially, Hilda's birthday was to fall on the sabbath, so I sat down to consider how best to celebrate the former while observing the latter. Knowing full well that what Hilda would enjoy more than anything was simply some time for just the two of us, I started making the arrangements. Though hardly the romantic type, I found myself looking forward to the prospect of spending much of my sabbath in the sole company of my wife, but even so, my mind was drawn back to the previous week and the holy leisure that I had felt more fully than ever before on the sabbath.

I began to wonder whether the sabbath was, after all, the right space for a romantic celebration. Perhaps the Puritans were right. Perhaps the 'sanctification' of the Lord's Day really could be accomplished only when all such matters were put aside on the sabbath. The Puritans who made their way to America became so convinced of this that couples found kissing on the sabbath were condemned and love-making on the Lord's day was denounced with great enthusiasm from the pulpit. One Massachusetts minister refused to baptize babies born on the sabbath, being fully convinced that children arriving on a Sunday must also have been conceived on one. At least, he refused until the Sunday when his wife bore the good Reverend a set of twins.[9]

The rabbis' view of *shabbat* could hardly have been more different from that of the Puritans who landed at Plymouth Rock. Instead of prohibiting marital relations on the sabbath, the rabbis of the Talmud actively encouraged them. In answer to the question of how often scholars should perform their conjugal duty, 'Rab Judah in the name of Samuel replied: Every Friday night. "That bringeth forth its fruit in its season" (Ps. 1:3), Rab Judah... stated: This [refers to the man] who performs his marital duty every Friday night.'[10] On a day when Jews are to mirror God's rest by abstaining from acts of creation, this encouragement to engage in the most creative act of all represents an exception both singular and significant. Evidently, for the rabbis at least, devotion to one's wife was not so much a distraction from the sabbath as a celebration of it.

With this in mind, and my mind at ease, we left baby Anna in the capable hands of her aunt and went out for a midwinter's dip in the outdoor hot springs at the city's spa hotel. We agreed not to talk about Anna for a change and instead spoke of everything and nothing as the steam rose from the surface into the clear, cold sky and our hair went white with frost. Only when we had wrinkled like prunes did we pull ourselves out of the pool and head downstairs to the restaurant, where we spent too much, drank a little and remembered what dinner had been like before high chairs and food fights.

Spending the whole of our sabbath or even part of it away from our daughter didn't feel like something we wanted to do very often, but I found myself enjoying, to an extent I had not anticipated, this rare opportunity to rest in the company of my wife without many of the usual distractions. It made me wonder whether the rabbis and the medieval Jewish mystics weren't right to speak of the sabbath as a 'bride'—the kind of partner who, when she arrives, is welcomed with the words of the Song of Solomon and the 16th-century song *Lekhah Dodi*, 'Come, my beloved'. This 'bride' deserves our undivided attention and devotion from the moment she appears until the hour when she takes her leave.

Eventually, and somewhat reluctantly, we paid our bill, collected our coats and left the restaurant behind. As we walked through the bright cold night, a part of me was looking forward to the broad smile of our one-year-old, which I knew would greet us when we got home. But at the same time, there was another part somewhere within me that wished we might have had a bit longer—a part that wished neither the sabbath nor the rest of Hilda's company had to come to an end at all. The rabbis would have understood this well, for they too found it difficult to say farewell to Queen Sabbath—which is why, after the sabbath itself is over each week, Jews for centuries have enjoyed the fellowship and festivities of the *melaveh malkah*, a gathering that sees 'Queen Sabbath' out for another week just as warmly as she is welcomed in.

+

Working words

Despite all the inspiring examples of sabbath keeping that I had discovered in my own seeking, there were times when I wondered whether, in various places and at various times, people had got a bit carried away. In the middle of the 17th century, a Massachusetts woman was prosecuted for allowing her Saturday brewing to continue during the sabbath, even though the only work being done was by the yeast. But of course the Puritans weren't the only people, or even the earliest, to devote themselves to detailing exactly what was forbidden on the sabbath. Even before the rabbis arrived at their list of 39 ways not to work on the sabbath, the Jewish tradition had pondered the question that the fourth commandment inevitably raised: 'What is the work from which we are to rest?' When, for example, Isaiah warned against 'speaking words' on the sabbath (58:13), did he really mean for there to be silence, or simply no 'idle talk', as many English versions suggest?

For the rabbis, the answer was obvious. For them, Isaiah had made it clear that 'thy speech [conversation] on the Sabbath should not be like thy speech on weekdays'.[11] 'Surely not!' I remember thinking when I first read it. Not working on the sabbath had seemed perfectly reasonable and turned out to be remarkably restful, but prohibiting weekday (inevitably workday) talk seemed excessive and quite unnecessary—that is, until one Sunday when I called up an acquaintance I hadn't spoken to in years.

We were friends from college days, but had lost touch as most people do, without meaning to. Before either of us had finished our studies, she had moved to another university and, when I finally left Scotland for a teaching post in Canada, that seemed to be that. But with a return trip to Scotland only days away, I decided that this was the time to give my old friend a call—if it didn't happen now, it probably never would. Separated by the Atlantic and several time zones, I reached her on what was my Sunday morning and her afternoon. As we began to catch up, her voice seemed sad—not despondent so much as resigned to some deep disappointment. It was hardly surprising, then, when she eventually admitted that she had separated from her husband in the years since we'd spoken. It had been too long and the wound was too deep for me to say much that I thought would make a difference. It was partly for this reason, and perhaps also because college was where we had met, that our conversation turned quickly to college life. Although she talked more about her job than I did about mine, it was enough to turn my thoughts to work and what needed to be done in the week ahead. We spoke for a few minutes more before making plans to chat again soon, and I rushed off to get ready for church.

Only in the middle of the sermon, as I sat in my pew, did I realize that although the morning's call had ended, the conversation hadn't. The fact that I had only myself for a conversation partner made little difference as I mulled over the work matters that should have been, and usually would have been, far from my mind on the sabbath. Instead of being fixed on the Lord whose day it was, my thoughts had been turned by my short conversation earlier that morning toward questions more appropriate to Monday than Sunday—or, in my case at least, more appropriate to Sunday evening than the Sunday service.

When you work with your hands for a living, doing that kind of work on the sabbath isn't always easy to keep a secret. But when you spend much of your time thinking for a living, however modest the thoughts, it is all too easy to work just as hard on Sunday as you would any other day. After all, no one needs to know. I can remember Sundays in my childhood when most of me sat apparently attentive in the pew while my mind was most definitely elsewhere. In those days, 'elsewhere' meant anywhere but work, but, as an adult, work was precisely where my mind was most prone to wander. Having wandered there, it wasn't always willing to be drawn back to holy leisure and the matters that should matter most on the Lord's Day. On this day, though, my mind was drawn back by the welcome distraction of food and fellowship as we gathered for Sunday lunch after the service at the house of some friends. Among them, there was little room for the thoughts of Monday morning as we shared and laughed and spoke of everything but work.

Later that week, when my friend in Scotland left a message suggesting that I call her back the following Sunday, I remembered another ancient text that we had both studied in our college days. The Jews who wrote it and preserved it in the caves alongside the Dead Sea were as strict about the sabbath as any other Jews of their time and considerably more so than many: 'And on the sabbath day, let no one speak a vain or empty word, nor press his fellow about any debt, nor let him judge concerning wealth or profit. Let him not speak concerning matters of craft or work to be done the next morning.'[12]

In the end, the Dead Sea Jews who weren't dispersed by the Romans were claimed by the dust of the desert itself, along with the texts they had written, but the words they left behind live on as a reminder that words are but a mirror of the mind. That's why, when I promised to return my friend's call, I resolved to do so not on the Lord's day but on the day before instead.

✛

30 January

A Methodist Mass

When my sister called this week to say that my dad had had a minor stroke, what frightened me most was the fact that I didn't feel more frightened. This was the first time either of my parents had suffered a health crisis worthy of the name, and the prospect should have been enough, I imagined, to strike fear into the heart of even the most distant and uninterested son—and I hoped I was neither.

It may have been the way my sister gently shared the news. The fact that Dad hadn't had a major stroke, merely a 'minor' one, certainly helped to allay my fears, and would have done even more so if I had better understood the difference. Exactly how minor it was became clear when I discovered that, shortly after being admitted, Dad was asking the same assistant who had found him in his office, incoherent and half-blind, to bring some files for him to work on from his hospital bed. Her refusal to do so (much to the relief of my mother) would have frustrated my father more, I'm sure, if he had been feeling more himself. But a stroke, even a minor one, is still a stroke, and when it is suffered by a father and a husband apparently in his prime, his family cannot help but feel the effect of it, so Hilda and I decided to pay my parents a visit at the weekend.

When we arrived on Saturday afternoon, Dad was nowhere to be found—or, rather, he was easily found as long as you knew where to look, which was not at home but in town at his office. When he eventually walked through the door, he looked absolutely fine and, when I asked him, he wasted no time in confirming that that was exactly how he felt. But I could see he was shaken, not so much by what had happened as by what might have happened if the stroke hadn't been so minor and help hadn't been so readily at hand.

As the afternoon wound down, my mother began to prepare dinner—rather early, I thought, until I remembered that my parents were in the habit of attending church on a Saturday evening instead of Sunday morning. For much of their church's recent history, Saturday evening had been reserved for the Catholic congregation next door, with whom they shared a car park. When the Methodists decided to begin meeting on Saturday night too, it wasn't because they wanted to celebrate the Mass. It was because the second Sunday morning service that was started when the first became full had itself become short of space. Unlike many Catholics and Jews who attend services both on the eve of their respective sabbaths and again the following morning, there was little point in my parents returning on Sunday because once you'd attended one service, it was as if you'd attended all three.

I knew of another church in our town that had decided to meet on a Saturday evening in the hope that those who weren't attending on Sunday morning might find the evening before more appealing. A friend who was involved there told me that the move to Saturday night hadn't made church more appealing to those who weren't already attending on Sunday. It had simply made it more convenient for the Christians who were attending on Sunday morning and wished they weren't. For the folk going to church on Saturday evening, Sunday morning became considerably more civilized. Instead of having to get up for Sunday school, there was time to sleep in, and without the service itself to attend, it was easy to beat the church crowd to Sunday lunch. In the eyes of some, this might well seem like the sabbath at its most restful, free from any encumbrance—except that the Lord's day, and eventually the Christian sabbath, never had been a rest from worship. Within the Christian tradition, Sunday seems to have

71

been first and foremost a day for worship and only later a day of rest as well.

There may have been some among the many who gathered with my parents and me for the service that evening who did so only for convenience, but even if they did, I suspect they were blessed in spite of it. Just like our Catholic neighbours were doing on the other side of the car park at about the same time, we welcomed the sabbath eve by taking Communion. Perhaps because these Methodists celebrated the eucharist far less frequently than their Catholic counterparts, there was, it seemed to me, an unusual sense of anticipation and expectation in the air as the service began. Our service was quite different in typically Protestant ways from the Mass taking place next door, but our respective celebrations of the central mystery of the Christian faith were the same to me in most of the ways that truly matter. Indeed, with the lights down low in the sanctuary, the bread and wine laid out and an abundance of candles, the atmosphere seemed rather more Roman than Methodist.

Curiously, though perhaps not surprisingly, many of the same elements play a part in the Jewish evening celebration of the sabbath—not in the gathering at the synagogue but in the home, both before and after the service. Before, the two candles, 'observe' and 'remember', are lit to herald the arrival of Queen Sabbath. Afterwards, on the family's return from the synagogue, traditional blessings are said over both wine and bread. Perhaps that's why, down through the centuries, the Jewish sabbath eve ritual has been seen by many as an anticipation of the Christian eucharist.

When the service was finished, my parents and I returned home to join the rest of the family for a rather more mundane ritual: dessert. In the midst of it, I found myself feeling profoundly thankful not only for the opportunity to mark the beginning of the Lord's day with the Lord's Supper, but also for the chance to do so in the company of a family I loved and a father whose presence I could no longer take for granted.

6 February

Time flies

Like the week before, I saw in this sabbath evening in the company of a crowd. After a short delay, the aircraft doors opened and we streamed down the aisles with the sole intent of discovering where we were sitting and, more importantly, beside whom. Expecting the worst, I was pleasantly surprised to find that my seat wasn't in the back row, as it often seemed to be, but only halfway back and with a clear view of the video screen. As I settled into my seat, the ones in front began to be filled and then those behind as well, until every last seat was taken—that is, all the cheap ones, which was all I could afford. In fact, from where I sat, I couldn't even see the swanky seats, the seats the rest of us walked past on our way to ours, the seats which in my weaker moments I had coveted because they looked so much more comfortable than my own. Comfortable is what you want be when you're going to be sitting for the better part of eight hours—and that's if you've got a tailwind. On the way back, the journey between the south of England and the west of Canada can sometimes take closer to ten.

I'd known all along that my ticket was for 5 February, but only later did I realize that the 5th would fall on a Saturday and that, by leaving in the evening, I would be setting out on my sabbath. By the time I had figured this out, it was far too late to do anything about it and I resigned myself to the fact that I would be spending this sabbath evening at 30,000 feet.

As I settled into my seat, I realized why, when you're crossing the Atlantic in economy class, comfort is a scarce commodity. It's no secret, of course—and certainly not to the airlines—but comfort is costly and, if you can't afford to fly first class, the truth is that most airlines can't really afford to keep you comfortable. Instead, they do their best to distract you, in the hope that, for a few hours at least, you'll forget how thin the blankets are and how disposable the pillows. Even with the steady stream of drinks and sandwiches, warm towels and feature films, I was finding it hard to forget that I was already far from home and getting farther away by the minute and that, somewhere back there, my little family was spending their sabbath evening catching up with a Christian couple whom Hilda hadn't seen in years. I wanted to be with them instead of where I was, so I did my best to shut out the dull roar of the engines, the hiss of the air conditioning above and the steady stream of chatter all around me. I wanted to pray but instead drifted off into a fitful sleep.

Exactly why long-haul air travel is so tiring is a bit of a mystery to me, particularly when there's little else to do but eat, drink and doze. Perhaps it's the inactivity itself that is so enervating and exhausting, or maybe it is the constant awareness that even when the lights go down for the 'evening' and a certain stillness settles over the cabin, you're still very much in motion, still travelling hundreds of miles per hour. Even though it's quiet on the inside, on the outside the world's flashing past faster than ever.

After we'd landed with a bump at Heathrow and while we were still taxiing to the gate, the captain announced the local time in London, confirming what was obvious to anyone with a window seat: our night had been too short and the morning had arrived too early. It dawned on me then that the seven hours I'd spent over the Atlantic weren't the only hours I'd lost. Another seven had slipped by as we raced east across the time zones from Mountain Standard all the way to Greenwich Mean, and I began to feel as if my sabbath was going to be over almost before it had begun.

It was Sunday morning, and as I walked through the already crowded terminal I wondered whether I might find a place to stop and pray or worship, even for a moment. But no sooner had the thought entered my mind than I remembered that our departure from Canada had been delayed. Instead of having ample time to make my connection, I now had virtually none, so instead of seeking out the airport chapel I hurried off in search of my flight to Scotland. When I got to the gate, I was out of breath but in luck. This flight too was delayed and so I made it with time to spare. Unfortunately, the same couldn't be said of my luggage, as I found out when I finally arrived up north.

What little was left of Sunday slipped away shortly after I landed in Scotland. Despite my best efforts to remember the sabbath, it had certainly not been a sabbath to remember—and I thought I knew why. When ancient Jews read Exodus 16:29, 'Let no man go out of his place on the seventh day' (RSV), they were sure that the words weren't just for Israel in the wilderness but for God's people in all times and in all places. Although the rabbis would later debate among themselves exactly how far was too far to travel on the sabbath, they would certainly have agreed with the ancient Jewish historian Josephus when he said that it is not 'lawful for us to journey, either on the Sabbath day or on a festival day'.[13] Having passed my entire sabbath doing exactly that, I decided that I wouldn't be doing so again any time soon, not because I wasn't permitted but because I was utterly persuaded that the way I had passed the day was no way to spend the sabbath.

✛

13 February

A sabbath sacrifice

It strikes some people as odd and perhaps even slightly ironic that while the majority of God's people are supposed to rest on the sabbath, the pastor, the priest and the rabbi have always found themselves busier than ever. In fact, the rabbis' later observation that 'the temple service takes precedence over the Sabbath'[14] was already so obvious by the time of Jesus that he was able to remind the Pharisees of it:

At that time Jesus went through the cornfields on the sabbath; his disciples were hungry, and they began to pluck heads of grain and to eat. When the Pharisees saw it, they said to him, 'Look, your disciples are doing what is not lawful to do on the sabbath.' He said to them, '… Have you not read in the law that on the sabbath the priests in the temple break the sabbath and yet are guiltless?' (Matthew 12:1–3a, 5)

Both Jesus and the Pharisees understood that according to Numbers 28, the priests' sacrificial duty, their role in keeping the people right with God, was something that could not be set aside on the sabbath—not if the people wanted God to be with them. The same has been true ever since, and while those of us who aren't in parish ministry might have a hard time appreciating it, it's something that my friend Nate understands full well, not because he's sending up burnt offerings but because he knows what it means to sacrifice on the sabbath.

Nate isn't just a friend, he's also a youth pastor in Mesa, Arizona, just outside Phoenix, which is where he ended up after we left Scotland and went our separate ways. Having spent the last few days in Edinburgh, where we'd studied together and worked together and prayed together years before, I found myself following in his footsteps as I made my way to Phoenix for a meeting with other Deans of colleges. As wonderful as it was to spend a few days with these godly men, most of whom seemed gifted in ways I felt I wasn't, it was still more of a blessing to spend a few hours with my friend.

Even though my hotel was a few minutes' drive from the airport and his home was miles away, Nate came to meet me at the airport because that's the kind of friend he is. He is also the kind of friend who gets so caught up in catching up with his friends that even though the journey to the hotel was only five minutes, it took 25 to get there. As tired as I was, it didn't seem to matter because it had been so long since I'd seen him and our time was so short.

A couple of days later, once the meetings were over, he returned to pick me up and take me out to where he lived and ministered. We sped along the highway, winding our way through the endless urban sprawl that had swallowed the desert in every direction. As we entered Mesa, Nate told me somewhat sheepishly that our afternoon had been spoken for and that we were headed not to his house but to the home of one of the kids in his youth group. They were shooting a home video for an event the following week and this was the only time when they could do it. Although I was in no shape to help him, and told him as much, I certainly didn't want to stand in the way either, so he suggested I tag along. I was glad I did, not because I had a part to play but because it was a blessing to see my friend in ministry. I must admit that the precise details of plot and character were lost on me, but if the kids who ended up watching it enjoyed it even half as much as did Nate and the kids who made it, then it will have been a great success.

By the time the video shoot was over, an unseasonably grey and wet Saturday afternoon was itself drawing to a close, but as we were backing out of the driveway, I discovered that our work was, in fact, just beginning. After stopping for supplies, we spent the next hour and a half on a driving tour of Mesa, not because there was anything remarkable or even especially attractive about this bit of suburbia but because in a few short minutes his kids were going on a citywide scavenger hunt and, if we didn't get the clues out soon, there were certain to be some very disoriented and disappointed hunters. As we drove from restaurants to monuments to goodness knows where else, I fought off a feeling of disappointment. This was not how I'd imagined us spending the few hours that I had with my friend. What's more, after one of the fullest weeks that I could remember, I had been looking forward to spending my sabbath evening relaxing over dinner.

Not a moment too soon, we arrived at the church, where a few teens were already waiting for the fun to begin. One by one, others began to appear until eventually a small crowd of kids stood in the middle of the car park, awaiting their instructions. Having divided them into teams and assigned them their drivers, Nate and I stood back and watched as they excitedly piled into the vehicles, raced out of the car park and sped into the night. Then we did the same, in the direction of a little taco shop not far from the church. It was a dingy place, dilapidated even, with spartan tables and the television turned up too loud, but the welcome was warm and the food absolutely delicious.

Over Mexican sodas and a few too many tacos, we talked about everything and nothing as friends do, but Nate also spoke of the sabbath and how difficult it is sometimes for those who serve God and his people to set aside time to be with him, or simply to be. Nate tried his best to set aside a day of the week other than Sunday, but sometimes his best wasn't good enough, because when you are working with kids in high school, the crises can't be pencilled in on your calendar. After what seemed like no time at all, we had to head back to the church to wait for the return of the teams. As we did, and I felt the sense of resentment beginning to return, I reminded myself that if my friend Nate was willing to serve these kids week in and week out, sacrificing a bit of my sabbath for their sake was the very least that I could do.

✛

20 February

Seeking justice

After being away for two weekends, one of the best things about being back home was being back at church. It wasn't perfect, our little church, but in a winter and a world that can sometimes seem pretty cold, it felt warmer than most. Unlike some other churches I'd attended, ours was small enough that when you missed a Sunday, someone noticed. Not everyone, of course, but enough to let you know that you had been missed, and that they were glad you were back.

One of the reasons I was especially glad to be back was that this week our church was welcoming a visiting speaker. When she walked up to the front, there wasn't much about her that seemed to stand out. She was smaller and a bit rounder than average and not particularly prepossessing. She was obviously reading from a prepared text and, though she spoke well enough, she was clearly less comfortable than many who found themselves up front at our church. It didn't take long, however, before I began to understand that what was outstanding about this woman was what she had to say, not how she said it. Her life had been radically transformed by the living God, and, from the sound of it, it was a good thing too, because if her life hadn't changed when it did, she had planned to end it herself. Without the prospect of work and caught in a marriage without love or the hope of finding it, the only thing she was living for was her children. So, with drugs to numb the pain during the week and drink to help her forget it at the weekend, she carried on until life itself seemed too much to bear and she became convinced that the world would be a better place, or at least no worse, without her. It was then, she told us, in the darkest of moments, that God brought a friend to her door who offered her something she thought she'd lost for ever: hope. Hope against hope that there might be a God out there who cared for someone as poor and depressed and doped-up as she was.

Her story didn't end there. It didn't end with her. First her husband and then her children began to follow God and it wasn't long before she became convinced that the God who had saved her was calling her to serve him by serving others. At first she was sure that the 'others' she was to serve were somewhere else, probably a long way away and potentially somewhere quite exotic. Instead, she discovered that the others who needed her most were those whose needs were most like her own, so she plunged into ministry almost on her doorstep, in an inner-city neighbourhood that she had been doing her best to get out of for as long as she could remember. The result was something called The Bridge, a place for people on the margins and especially for those who were on the edge and about to fall over it. It started as a safe place to get a bowl of soup but soon became a kind of community centre where the centre of the community was Christ and the people who came found it hard to leave.

As she spoke, I glanced around at the people in the pews. All eyes were fixed on this unassuming woman, and the congregation as a whole seemed on the edge of its collective seat, ears straining to take everything in and savouring this story of transformation as if it were their own. But of course it wasn't, and that was also perhaps why most of our middle-class congregation listened so attentively. The woman's story was safe because most of us had never been down a road quite as dark as hers, and inspiring in the way that stories are when they are set somewhere else—because 'somewhere else' the people are always much more needy than where we are.

Our congregation was, in fact, pretty comfortable with itself, friendly to a fault and quite content to keep the home fires of Free

Methodism burning in our little town well into the 21st century. Most of the folks were even quite good and probably better than me at keeping some sort of sabbath, whether because they felt they should or because, like me, they felt that it did them good. But as I mulled this over in my mind, I began to wonder whether we weren't a bit like the people of God in the prophet Isaiah's time, a people who, when they heard his words, must have been cut to the quick:

Bring no more vain offerings; incense is an abomination to me. New moon and sabbath and the calling of assemblies—I cannot endure iniquity and solemn assembly. Your new moons and your appointed feasts my soul hates; they have become a burden to me, I am weary of bearing them. When you spread forth your hands, I will hide my eyes from you; even though you make many prayers, I will not listen; your hands are full of blood. Wash yourselves; make yourselves clean; remove the evil of your doings from before my eyes; cease to do evil, learn to do good; seek justice, correct oppression; defend the fatherless, plead for the widow. (Isaiah 1:13–17, RSV)

The woman's words were a welcome reminder to me and, I hoped, to any others who needed reminding that keeping the sabbath is not enough and it never had been—not in Moses' time, not in Isaiah's time, not even when Christ himself walked this earth. According to Isaiah, to keep the sabbath without correcting oppression, without defending the fatherless and without pleading for the widow wasn't only unfair to them, it was actually offensive to God. This same God sent his Son to remind us that if remembering the sabbath causes us to forget the needs of our neighbour, we would be better off not remembering the sabbath at all.

✛

27 February

Shabbat Shalom

Although a warm spell in the heart of a prairie winter is a welcome respite, anyone from round these parts knows that the inevitable return of the cold often turns pavements into skating rinks. If it were possible to skate down the street, this might well be fine and perhaps even fun, but it's neither when a trip along the road invariably involves a slip of some sort or another. Unfortunately, the sort of slip our friend had suffered was more serious than most, so at the first available moment the doctors decided to operate. She didn't seem particularly old to me, but Lee was at the age where any kind of surgery was serious and any recovery bound to be far too slow for her liking. But thanks to regular updates from her husband, we heard that the operation went well—or as well as could be expected when you're replacing an entire hip—and that she was headed home to recover there under his watch and care.

We knew both Lee and her husband from the community ministry we were involved with and, though we weren't especially close, the more familiar they had become to us, the fonder we had become of them. Maybe that's why our failure to visit Lee began to bother me. My conscience was salved somewhat by the news, again from her husband, that many had been by to see her even if I hadn't, and there was some perverse reassurance to be found in the fact that I had never really been the sort to spend much time visiting folk uninvited. The reason was that I was convinced that visiting people would require me to spend not just a little but a lot of time, and, for years now, I had felt as if I didn't have a lot of time to spend. In fact, I was sure that I barely had any time at all to spend—that if time was something you kept in a bank, I was pretty much broke. As I had gradually begun to recover something of my lost sabbath, though, this feeling had begun to fade, slowly at first, but now to the point where I may not have had a lot of time, but I did have a little, and on this sabbath we decided to spend at least some of it with Lee and her husband.

After a midwinter's walk alongside the little river that winds its way through our town, we beat a hasty retreat from the icy paths and a few minutes later were happy to find Lee and her husband at home and the patient in good spirits. Ensconced on a sofa-bed in her living-room with a walking-frame close at hand, she seemed tired but as pleased to see us as we were to see her. As we talked, it became clear that the steady stream of visitors who had called while she was in the hospital had been a real blessing to them both. They took particular pride in telling us that one of the older couples in the church had been so committed to visiting Lee in the hospital each Sunday that they showed up even after she'd been discharged. So intent were they on their sabbath visit that they checked to see if she'd been moved to another hospital, before eventually discovering that she had been sent home. This couple's persistence in visiting his wife on the sabbath didn't surprise Lee's husband, because that's how it had always been when he was growing up. After all, when you're farming six days a week, there's not a lot of time left over for visiting except on the sabbath, when the work of the week is set aside.

The idea of spending at least part of the sabbath visiting those who are under the weather is hardly a new one, of course. In the early 19th century, the Revd Daniel Wilson, one of the founders of the Lord's Day Observance Society, suggested 'visiting the sick and needy' as one of many worthwhile ways to pass at least part of the Christian sabbath.[15] Long before evangelical Protestants or their Catholic counterparts had latched on to the idea, the rabbis were well aware of the importance of visiting the sick. Some, like Rabbi Simeon, thought that the trauma of doing so was too much like work to be suitable for the sabbath. Undoubtedly that's why the *Magen Avraham*, a medieval commentary, suggests that Jews should visit the sick on the sabbath only if it can't be done on any other day of the week. Over the centuries, though, most Jews, including the great Maimonides, came to see paying a visit to someone who was ill as precisely the sort of thing that should be done on *shabbat*. This is why, according to the Talmud, 'Our Rabbis taught: If one enters to visit a sick person, he should say, "It is the Sabbath when one must not cry out, and recovery will soon come".'[16]

Although our friend knew full well that the road to recovery was certain to include twists and turns, the look on her face as she sat on her sofa-bed suggested that relief was indeed drawing nigh and that, in the midst of family and friends, there was less cause to cry than there might have been. Her condition had prevented her from coming to church on Sundays, but it was clear that the church had come to her instead since she'd been laid up and, more often than not, folk came on the sabbath.

I'm not sure whether it was because, on this sabbath, we were her only visitors or because she was obviously on the mend and in good spirits, but I was especially glad that we'd decided to drop by. It certainly didn't feel like work. In fact, instead of distressing or depressing me, spending my sabbath visiting a friend in her struggles was a wonderful reminder of God's provision not only of rest, but also of restoration. And so, instead of the warning of Rabbi Simeon, I found myself lingering on the words of Rabbi Shebna, words that he offered when he arrived at a sickbed on the sabbath and again when he departed, words that cling to the sabbath wherever and whenever Jews greet each other on the day of rest: *Shabbat Shalom*.

✢

In Daddy's arms

With a toddler in the house, most of my sabbath mornings began the same way: a bit earlier than I would have wished. Unlike our alarm clock, our little girl didn't come with a snooze button. Although some mornings began in tears, when I poked my head through the doorway on this morning she was all smiles, which seemed a sure sign that she was not only more wide awake than I was but rather more happy about it, too.

Before we had one of our own, I really did find babies infinitely resistable, but now that I was a dad, I was as entranced as everyone else—and never more so than when my little girl was all smiles, as she was this morning. I remember, when I was a teenager, wondering why anyone would want even one baby, let alone more than one. Now I know: it's the smile. It's the smile that makes babies so attractive and probably at least partly why, for many parents, having them is so addictive. It's the smile you get when you arrive home from work after a long day at the office—the kind of smile that convinces you that no one has ever been as happy to see you as your child is, but also that it's only a matter of time before the novelty wears off and she'll realize I'm just her dad.

On this morning, though, with her mother dozing in bed, she was still very much Daddy's girl; and on this morning, as on every other, Daddy's girl needed her nappy.changed and her breakfast prepared. But having completed those tasks, and with her mother still asleep, the more pressing question became: what would we do, Anna and I, with our sabbath morning? There was the television, of course, that great friend of fathers down through the years, but, in a moment of moral fortitude or perhaps plain madness, I had promised Hilda that I would turn on the television only as a last resort—a promise that might have been harder to keep if Anna had shown much interest in it in the first place. There were also the toys, which, despite our best efforts, seemed to have multiplied over recent months to fill the small trunk in which we tried—and failed—to keep them. Many of them, and particularly some of the favourites, seemed dead set against staying in that trunk for any length of time and much preferred to be underfoot or generally in the way. On this Sunday, though, Anna toddled past them all and the television, too, toward the small rack of books that stood by the fireplace. Of the many books she might have picked out, it was the big red baby's Bible that she chose, so, with the book on her lap and Anna on mine, we settled on to the sofa and began to read.

We began, as we always did, in the beginning, and Anna waited patiently as God created the heavens and the earth for the umpteenth time. Turning the page, we read that when God had finished his creating, he rested—which, given how early it was and how sleepy I was, seemed a singularly good idea. When I looked down, however, the page had already been turned again, with the obvious implication that I should keep on reading—not about Cain, who was carefully passed by along with his brother, but about Noah and his rainbow. Despite my best efforts to interest Anna in the ark, the page soon turned once more and Noah was forgotten for the sake of Joseph, and then Moses and the Israelites. Before they could be redeemed, I found myself staring at a rather juvenile Samson, and 30 seconds later Jesus had been born.

This was 'reading' only in the loosest sense of the word, of course, not so much because of what we were reading but how we were reading it. Already abridged for the benefit of young eyes and ears, the Bible became increasingly condensed as we read. The further we went, the faster we went, and the result was a version that no one, including the publishers, had ever envisioned. For Anna, the fun seemed to lie in seeing how fast she could go, and I half wondered whether she had already caught the bug—the virus that drives us faster, longer and harder than we ought to go. This disease is carried by our culture but also passed on to us, often unwittingly, by our parents. One way or another, parents always pass things on to us. Why else would God remind his people, 'These commandments that I give you today are to be upon your hearts. Impress them on your children. Talk about them when you sit at home and when you walk along the road, when you lie down and when you get up. Tie them as symbols on your hands and bind them on your foreheads. Write them on the doorframes of your houses and on your gates' (Deuteronomy 6:6–9).

With a country to conquer and a land to bring to life, perhaps the commandment to rest would have been the most difficult for the Israelites to keep, and, as with all the other commandments, the only way for them to give the gift of rest to their children and ensure that they received it was to rest themselves. I knew that the same was true for me and my daughter as we sat on the sofa on this sabbath morning.

As the day wore on, though, I began to suspect that what I had only begun to learn about the sabbath, my daughter already knew while she was still in nappies. Most of her sabbath was spent playing with this toy or that doll, but after a while, every so often, she would stop what she was doing and toddle to where I sat reading on the sofa. After a few of these visits, I began to see that she came not because she needed my help or wanted anything much in particular. No, she came because, in the midst of her play, she wanted and perhaps even needed to rest for a moment in her father's arms. She needed to know that I was there, that she could just drop her own kind of busyness, climb up, cuddle up and rest her head on my shoulder. Each time she toddled back to her toy blocks, I marvelled at what my daughter was teaching me, marvelled at the goodness of God as I caught a glimpse of what our Father must feel as his children return to enjoy his creation, having taken the time to rest even for a moment in his arms.

✣

A day of prayer

When Constantine finally decided, in the fourth century, to make Sunday a day of rest as well as a day of worship, it wasn't just for the sake of the pious. It was also for the pagans, whether they liked it or not. In Sunday, even the cursing, swearing soldiers of the emperor's army were encouraged to meet to worship if they wished, and to pray even if they didn't wish. Perhaps because they were pagans, Constantine told them not only when to pray but also what to pray—a prayer that ended up being at least as much for his sake as for theirs: 'Together we pray to thee [O God], and beseech thee long to preserve to us, safe and triumphant, our emperor Constantine and his pious sons.'[17]

The days of prescribing prayer for those outside the faith are long gone, but it's equally true that for Christians and Jews down through the ages, the sabbath has long been a day of prayer. It's a day of prayer for creation, prayer for God's people and, as Pope Gregory reminded his flock in the sixth century, prayer for forgiveness: 'On the Lord's day... there should be a cessation of earthly labour, and attention given in every way to prayers so that if anything is done negligently during the six days, it must be expiated by supplications on the day of the Lord's resurrection.'[18]

With Anna heading off to bed just after supper, our sabbath too began with supplications, but of a rather different sort. Coming as they did in that strange, sleepy moment just after storytime and right before bed, the prayers we offered up on a sabbath evening were usually too short to be very sweet. They were prayers less for expiation than protection, for family, for friends, for ourselves and especially for our little girl. On this evening, though, as we tucked her in, said our prayers and turned off the light, I realized that I had been missing out. It dawned on me that in my search for rest, prayer ought to be an integral part of the process. It wasn't enough to pray simply *that* I would rediscover the sabbath; I needed to pray *in order* to rediscover the sabbath.

Thanks to my wife, the next morning, instead of getting up early with Anna, I got to sleep in. Perhaps because it so seldom happened any more, on Sunday or any other day, I felt a nagging sense of guilt in the middle of my morning grogginess, as if earliness was next to godliness, and I ought to get up sooner rather than later. Then I remembered that the rabbis saw the sabbath morning quite differently: they saw it as the perfect time (perhaps because it was the only time) to sleep a little later than usual.[19] If, however, sabbath morning has often been a time to sleep in and savour what the rabbis call the *oneg shabbat*, the pleasure of the sabbath, it has always been a time to pray along with the Psalms— the song book but also the prayer book of God's people, both Jewish and Christian, down the centuries.

Reaching for the Bible near our bed, I turned to the psalms that have traditionally spoken to God's people on the sabbath. There was Psalm 19, with its declaration of the goodness of God's world and the word by which he 'revives the soul' (v. 7); Psalm 34 and its opening promise, bold because of the times of pain and darkness that come to us all: 'I will bless the Lord at all times; his praise shall continually be in my mouth' (v. 1); and the plea of Moses in Psalm 90 that God would 'teach us to number our days that we may get a heart of wisdom' (v. 12, RSV). But among the many psalms that spoke truly to me and for me this sabbath morning, Psalm 92 spoke more clearly than the rest, just as it has for other people since it was composed in ancient times: 'A Psalm. A Song for the Sabbath Day. It is good to give thanks to the Lord, to sing praises to your name, O Most High; to declare your stead-fast love in the morning, and your faithfulness by night, to the music of the lute and the harp, to the melody of the lyre' (vv. 1–3).

Whether the author of the psalm wrote it for the sabbath or whether someone else read it and thought he did, the words became both my prayer and my plan for the rest of the day. As the sunlight shone through the still-bare branches of the great tree outside our window and filled the room, I was filled with a deep sense of gratitude and of the goodness of giving thanks to God. I felt a great desire to declare his love not only in the morning and his faithfulness at night, but also in every moment in between, which is what the Hebrew in its own poetic way means to say. So there alone in my room, I started to do exactly that, declaring how remarkable, faithful and loyal God's love for me really is. I was proclaiming it not to myself, but to him—not because he needed to hear it, of course, but because I did.

And so it continued, this sabbath prayer, off and on all day. At church, I prayed to music that would have seemed strange to the psalmist but, to me, seemed just right. As our minister preached, I prayed for another pastor I knew who was struggling in ministry. At home, I prayed over our lunch, realizing that although I seldom forget to eat during the week, I often forget to be thankful for it. In the afternoon, I prayed for a couple we knew who could neither bear to be apart nor figure out how to live together. None of my prayers was especially long, and certainly none was particularly profound, but they were a start—the start of a conversation that I hoped would extend beyond the sabbath, a conversation that, in the midst of my busyness, could only really have begun on the sabbath.

Palm Sunday in Portadown

Growing up in my church, 'lent' was what you found at the bottom of your pocket, not what you observed in the days leading up to Easter. But if Lent was largely unknown to us, the same could not be said of Palm Sunday, which we celebrated with great enthusiasm. Given the lack of palm trees on the Canadian prairies, our Sunday school teachers were forced to improvise year after year, arming us with various artificial alternatives or, when supplies were short, even cardboard which we had coloured ourselves. Until I grew old enough to be embarrassed by it, the prospect of parading up the aisle with the rest of the children, singing and waving our 'palms' dangerously close to our neighbours' heads, filled me with great joy. Although we sang the song 'This is the day' on many a Sunday, the words of Psalm 118:24, 'This is the day that the Lord has made, we will rejoice and be glad in it', never seemed more fitting than on the Sunday which was, for me as a child, the most joyful of them all. Because we celebrate the coming of the Messiah on Palm Sunday, there are few words more joyful than the words that follow in Psalm 118, the same words that would eventually follow Jesus that first Sunday of Palms as he entered Jerusalem: '*Hoshianna*, Save us… Blessed is the one who comes in the name of the Lord' (vv. 25–26).

On this Palm Sunday, though, it wasn't my childhood memories that we were revisiting—it was Hilda's. We awoke in her old room in her father's house on the outskirts of Portadown, as we usually did on our visits to Northern Ireland. Over the years, my trips to

Ulster had taught me that the sun seldom visited this land, or at least that its visits seldom seemed to coincide with mine. So it wasn't entirely surprising that this morning dawned only reluctantly, grey and dull and the hills heavy with mist, but on this day of all days, on the day when we greet the Son, I had hoped to be greeted by the sun.

Undeterred by the gloom of the morning, we went out to Sunday morning meeting because, as Quakers, that's what Hilda's family had always done. Although George Fox and the other Quakers of the 17th century resisted the legalism of the Puritan sabbath, they had soon recognized the practical benefit of a day of rest and the opportunity it offered them to meet for worship.[20] Over the years, I had come to love the little redbrick meeting house with its bare walls and its earnest sincerity. Though few in number, the Quakers who met there ensured that there was always a meeting, even if there were not many to meet. But on this day, part of me yearned for something else. I wanted to shout out loud. I wanted celebration and songs and several hundred people with which to enjoy them. What I didn't want was the silence that I knew would descend on the meeting as it always did, as we waited for God's Spirit to move someone to minister.

We waited—and we did not wait in vain. God's Spirit did move among those who were gathered there, knitting together the words, prayers and psalms that were offered so that they covered us all with God's grace. We were few in number and the words were spoken quietly, but there was a sense of celebration in our midst as we shared and heard things that ministered to our hearts. In the silence, the words of the psalm and the song began to resonate within me: 'This is the day, this is the day that the Lord has made, that the Lord has made. We will rejoice, we will rejoice and be glad in it, and be glad in it.' And as they resonated within my soul, I wondered whether they might not resound in more than just mine, and so, without thinking about why I shouldn't, I found myself suggesting that we sing this song together. We were not a large choir but our voices, some young and some old, some strong and some weak, were filled with the joy of those who have welcomed Christ into the city of their hearts.

As we finished singing and the voices fell silent, I was reminded that although Palm Sunday has always been filled with particular joy, every Sunday from the very beginning was to be a day of which to say, 'This is the day that the Lord has made', a day in which to be glad and rejoice. It's no wonder that the *Didascalia*, that ancient handbook of practical piety, reminded the early Christians, 'On the first day of the week make good cheer at all times.'[21] Nor is it surprising that St Augustine advised against penitence, fasting or even kneeling on the Christian sabbath, and instead urged the singing of the 'Alleluia' on Sunday.[22]

After the meeting, we returned to the house, and when we arrived I noticed that it was not only my mood that had brightened, but also the morning itself. The sun, having burnt off the mist, now beat down on the lush green hills and the countryside seemed to pulse with life. As I wandered near the house, my eyes were drawn to a bed of tulips and I stopped and bent down to take a closer look. Irridescent in the sunlight and almost more yellow than the sun itself, the tulip seemed a herald of spring and a harbinger of the holy season to come. As I marvelled at the beauty of it, the six perfectly formed petals and the pistil that stood at their centre seemed to me to be creation's own picture of the week. In this picture, the sabbath does not stand at the end of the week or even at its beginning, but at the centre of them all. It is not simply a day like all the rest, but a day in which we actually like to rest—a day in which we truly long to rest in the joy of knowing not only that 'this is the day that the Lord has made' but also that the sabbath has been made for humankind and not humankind for the sabbath.

Discovering the Lord's day

Although we were back in Canada in good time the following week, by Sunday I was running on empty. Remembering that I had agreed to preach not once but twice on Good Friday, and that there was much to be done before then, my mind had raced back from Ireland before we'd even stepped on to the plane to depart. When we stepped off it late that evening, though, my body felt as if it had missed one of our several connections and was still somewhere over the Atlantic. By the time everything finally caught up with me, the calendar informed me that it was already Friday.

Given the busyness of the week, I hadn't planned on being up before the sun on Easter morning, but once I was, and before anyone else was, I decided to make the best of it and go for a walk. In the chill, grey light of the dawn, the streets were still and the silence broken only by the chirrup of the robins from their rooftop perch. By the time I turned for home, the sun had emerged from its slumber and begun to peek between the trees and tall old houses of the neighbourhood. First southward and then eastward, then southward again, I zigged and zagged through the empty streets toward home. Each time I turned eastward, I turned toward the sun as it rose, and the higher it climbed, the brighter it seemed to burn. After a few minutes of travelling east, I was dazzled, almost blinded by the sun and it was only when I turned away, toward the south, that the colours of the world returned. Just as my eyes adjusted, my road would take me back toward the east and I would be blinded once more by the sheer intensity of the morning sun.

At it had done the previous week on Palm Sunday, half a world away, the risen sun on this Easter morning seemed to speak of and proclaim another Son—a Son who also rose on a morning long ago but in other ways perhaps not so very different from this one. While other Christian holy days are allowed to fall wherever they may in the week, Easter has been celebrated on Sunday since the earliest days of the Church, and perhaps even since the very beginning. Polycrates, a bishop of Ephesus in the second century, argued that Christians should celebrate Easter on the 14th of Nisan when the Jews celebrated Passover, but Christendom eventually sided with his Roman counterpart, Victor, preferring to celebrate it on the nearest Sunday instead.[23] Some have even suggested that it was the celebration of Easter on Sunday once a year that eventually led to Christians observing the Lord's day once a week. If it did, it would hardly be surprising, for the first Easter was certainly a Sunday and the Christian sabbath has been ever since, and at its heart, a celebration of the resurrection.

As I made my way home on this sabbath morning which was also Easter morning, I felt not just the joy of Palm Sunday, the joy of the coming Lord, but also the exultation of Easter, the joy of the risen Lord. It was a joy so overwhelming that, like the sun, it was too bright to be endured for long. When I finally arrived home, the house had awakened, and it was as if I was turning to the south, to a colourful, lively and lovely world bathed in the light of the risen Son but not blinded by it. Later in the morning, when we went to worship at the church, though, it was as if I had turned eastward once more, dazzled by the Light which had returned on the third day as we celebrated the resurrection of God himself on this the first day of the week. We returned home after the service and, as we prepared for the arrival of family and friends, I noticed the sun again, much higher now in the sky, its rays streaming through the window and illuminating the white tiles on the floor. It seemed as if, on this day, the whole world was reflecting the light of the risen Lord.

In the midst of it all, I thought back to Good Friday and an encounter I'd had with a man I'd never met before. Our paths crossed in the foyer after the service and, when he recognized me as the preacher, he grasped my hand and gave it the kind of shake which reminded me that some folks still work with their hands for a living, even if I don't. He thanked me earnestly for my sermon and then, to my chagrin but not entirely to my surprise, proceeded to make a point that left me wondering whether he'd heard much of it at all. Instead of the gore of Good Friday, I had spoken of the goodness of Friday and of the importance of not confusing it with the goodness of Easter Sunday. Whether the man had forgotten what day it was or had simply decided to ignore the fact, his words had little to do with Friday and everything to do with Sunday. What he said was this: 'Every Sunday should be Easter.' At the time, I was so frustrated that he had missed my point that I managed entirely to miss the significance of his—until two days later, which is when I realized that his point was the same as that of Pope Innocent I, who wrote to Bishop Decentius of Gubbio in the 5th century to remind him that 'we celebrate Sunday because of the venerable resurrection of our Lord Jesus Christ, not only at Easter but every Sunday'.[24]

'Every Sunday should be Easter.' After six months of seeking a sabbath I had lost, these words rang as true as any I'd heard and more true than most. In the unrelenting busyness of life, I had begun my search for the sabbath out of necessity, out of a need to make it through the next year, month or even week. I began my search understanding that humans were not made for the sabbath, but that the sabbath was made for humans and that therefore it was made for me—not for the sake of my salvation, but for the sake of my sanity.

As I looked back over the past few months, however, it occurred to me that the sabbath I had begun to recover and, in many ways, rediscover wasn't just made for me. It was made for my wife and my daughter, my family and my friends, and perhaps even my faculty at the theological college. The discipline of *shabbat*, of God-given rest from the work of the week and the world, had been all the blessing I had hoped for and incalculably more. But while this blessing began with the recovery of a day made for me, it ended with the discovery of a day which I saw must be devoted to him. It was to be a day of rest from everything except rejoicing in the love and the light of the risen Lord, a day not simply of ceasing but one of praising, and a day that is not simply the sabbath, but a day that must be first and foremost the Lord's day.

'Every Sunday should be Easter.' As the man's words rang in my ears, I began to realize that, after months of searching, this day that had been lost had, at some unfixable point along the way, become a day that had been found. But even as I rejoiced in my discovery, I recognized that in the maelstrom of life, this day that had, by God's grace, finally been found might easily be lost again if I allowed myself to forget the things I had learned when, for six months one year, I set out to seek the sabbath.

Epilogue

In the year that followed my search, I discovered that it's one thing to find the sabbath and quite another thing to keep it. I knew that if I wanted to keep the sabbath I'd rediscovered, I'd need to keep it the way that Deuteronomy encourages us to: I'd need to guard it, keep it safe and sound. I'd need to keep my eye on it so that it wouldn't go missing like it had before. But then I imagined that that wouldn't be difficult, given where God was taking us.

After a great deal of prayer and soul-searching and much to my own surprise, I accepted the invitation to become Principal of Belfast Bible College. Although I knew that leaving behind family, friends and our 'little house on the prairie' would be far from easy, I consoled myself with the thought that it would surely be easy to keep my rediscovered sabbath safe in a place like Northern Ireland. We were leaving small-town Saskatchewan behind for bustling Belfast, but I'd visited often enough over the years to know that, compared with Canada and indeed almost any country, the culture in Northern Ireland was as Christian as it could be. Among the Protestants at least, I was sure that Sunday would be safe, thanks to the theological predispositions of the Presbyterians, and, however violently they might disagree with their Catholic brethren about various issues important and irrelevant, I felt certain that Sunday was one subject on which Christians would see eye to eye. And so they did, but not in the way I expected.

I discovered that, much more than in Canada, though not as much as in the past, folk in Ulster did still find their way to church. For many, however, worship service apart, Sunday turned out to be little more than a day to do whatever hadn't been done during the week. It is a day when some shops are closed but, as soon as church is finished, the supermarket is busier than ever— a day when the peal of church bells at the end of the lane is increasingly drowned out by the roar of power tools next door.

After a few months as Principal, I also discovered that my new job was no less busy than my old one. There were not only new students to teach, new staff to get to know, but also a new college to lead. What made things even busier was that there was also a constituency to reassure and a wider college community with whom I needed to connect, and Sunday seemed to be the traditional day to do both. Sunday soon started to seem like the only day left to prepare that lecture or mow the lawn or fix that shower. Almost without my noticing it, the day that I'd rediscovered, the sabbath that God had graciously restored to my life, began to slip away again.

As much as I tried to justify my Sunday plumbing, as much as I tried to sanctify that cursed shower for the sake of the sabbath, I simply couldn't, in the end, bear the thought of losing what I'd discovered over the previous months. I was unwilling to forget what had become for me, my family and my relationship with God, a truly sacred space in our week.

My own near miss was a reminder to me that if busy people want to keep the sabbath, we must be ready to guard it. The bad news is that because an increasingly non-Christian society in the West seems willing to safeguard the sabbath only so long as it doesn't stand in the way of its commercial purposes, we shouldn't expect much help from that quarter. The good news is that we shouldn't need society's help. If Jews like my friends, Willem and Marian, can keep the Orthodox *shabbat* with all its *mitzvot* in the midst of the multicultural melting pot of London, surely we as Christians can keep an eye on the sabbath for the sake of our own sanity. Ironically, as our society keeps the sabbath less and as we do so more, Christians will become, in one way at least, like our Jewish brothers and sisters, a people set apart. Indeed, it may be that as we set apart the 'rest' of God, others will be pointed toward the 'rest of God'.

Although it is increasingly obvious that the world around us will refuse to stop for a minute, let alone a day, the greatest danger against which we must safeguard the sabbath is not from outside, but from within. The gate to the sabbath, the gate that we must guard, is not to be found at the local supermarket; it is to be found deep within ourselves. It is there that we feel the pressure to do and do and do some more, and it is there that the pressures of this world beat upon the door. It's there that the decision is taken to fling open the gates to the business and busyness that fills our lives. It's there that the watch must be kept with care, just as it was at the gates of Jerusalem in the time of the Persians. In Nehemiah's time, it was not enough simply to bar the door once and for all against the forces of 'unrest'; he tells us in his memoirs that he detailed some to continually 'guard the gates, to keep the sabbath day holy' (Nehemiah 13:22) And so too must we, if we wish to keep the sabbath, mount a constant guard at the gates of our heart against our own relentless refusal to rest.

Notes

1   Codex Justinianus, III, 12, 3; English translation Philip Schaff, *History of the Christian Church*, Vol. 3 (5th ed.; Scribner, 1902), p. 380, note 1.

2   Nicolas Bownde, *Sabbathum Veteris et Novi Testamenti: Or the True Doctrine of the Sabbath* (London, 1606), p. 148.

3   Epistle of Barnabas, Ch. XV; English translation J.B. Lightfoot, *The Apostolic Fathers* (Macmillan and Co., 1891).

4   Gregory the Great, *Homilies on Ezekiel*, Hom. 2; English translation Samuele Bacchiocchi, *From Sabbath to Sunday* (Pontifical Gregorian University, 1977), p. 295.

5   R. Wurmbrand, *Sermons in Solitary Confinement* (Marshall Morgan & Scott, 1984; originally published by Hodder & Stoughton in 1969), p. 121.

6   Babylonian Talmud (Soncino): Avodah Zarah 3a.

7   Babylonian Talmud (Soncino): Shabbat 119a.

8   Thomas Merton, *Spiritual Direction and Meditation* (The Liturgical Press, 1960), p. 74.

9   Winton U. Solberg, *Redeem the Time: The Puritan Sabbath in Early America* (Harvard University Press, 1977), p. 114.

10 Babylonian Talmud (Soncino): Ketubot 62b.

11 Babylonian Talmud (Soncino): Shabbat 113a–b.

12 Damascus Document col. X, 17–18, trans. F. Garcia Martinez, *The Dead Sea Scrolls Translated*, 2nd ed. (Brill, 1996).

13 Flavius Josephus, *Antiquities of the Jews* Bk XIII, Ch. 8, Sec. 4; English translation William Whiston (Lea, 1850).

14 Babylonian Talmud (Soncino): Shabbat 132b.

15 Daniel Wilson, *The Divine Authority and Perpetual Obligation of the Lord's Day, asserted in seven sermons* (London, 1831).

16 Babylonian Talmud (Soncino): 12a

17 *Life of Constantine* (Eusebius) Chs. XVIII–XX, Nicene and Post-Nicene Fathers Vol. 1 (2nd Series) (Repr. Eerdmans, 1955).

18 *To the Romans* (Gregory the Great) Epistle 1, Nicene and Post-Nicene Fathers Vol. XIII (Eerdmans, 1955).

19 Orach Chayim 281 (Shulchan Aruk). Justified on the basis of Numbers 28:4 (morning) and 9 (sabbath day).

20 Indeed, William Penn's American Quakers were initially very keen observers of the Lord's Day and required complete rest from sports and work.

21 *Didascalia Apostolorum*, Ch. XXI, trans. R.H. Connolly (Clarendon Press, 1929), p. 192.

22 *To Januarius* (Augustine) Epistle LV, Ch. XV, Nicene and Post-Nicene Fathers, Vol. I (1st Series) (Repr. Eerdmans, 1955).

23 For an ancient discussion of the controversy, see Eusebius of Caesarea, *History of the Church*, Bk V, XXIII–XXV Nicene and Post-Nicene Fathers, Vol. I (2nd Series) (Repr. Eerdmans, 1955).

24 Innocent I, *Ad Decentium*, Epist. 25, 4, 7, PL 20 555; trans. Samuele Bacchiocchi, *From Sabbath to Sunday* (Pontifical Gregorian University, 1977), 205.

Driven Beyond the Call of God

Discovering the rhythms of grace

Pamela Evans

'In attempting to serve the church and our neighbour with all our hearts, minds and strength, we can find ourselves sucked into a lifestyle which undermines our very purpose and makes nonsense of our message.'

This powerful book shows how, rather than presenting the good news, 'church' can sometimes be very bad news indeed. Christians may find themselves driven towards burn-out, becoming so absorbed in the process of worshipping and serving God that they lose sight of him altogether.

Drawing on years of pastoral experience, the author explores a right view of God and shows how his true requirements of us actually produce good mental and spiritual health. She shows, too, how we need an experience of his grace—a gift we cannot earn, however hard we try. A helpful study section encourages us to reflect on the pace, direction and motivation of our lives, and work with others towards a healthier style of discipleship.

ISBN 1 84101 054 5 £7.99
Available from your local Christian bookshop or, in case of difficulty, direct from BRF using the order form on page 111.

A Fruitful Life

Abiding in Christ as seen in John 15

Tony Horsfall

'It is my desire through these pages to point you back to the simplicity of a life lived out of relationship with Jesus Christ. A life of intimacy, of abiding in him, is the source and spring of all other activity and endeavour. The branch bears fruit because it abides in the vine.'

In *A Fruitful Life* we ponder the teaching of Jesus in John 15, the famous 'vine' passage. He is preparing his disciples for his departure and describing how they can be effective witnesses in a hostile world. Just as his instructions revolutionized their lives, so a proper understanding of what he is saying can revolutionize our lives also. It is the heart of the gospel message: the only way to live the Christian life is to allow Jesus to live his life in us and through us.

This book includes material for individual reflection and also questions for group discussion.

ISBN 1 84101 335 8 £6.99
Available from your local Christian bookshop or, in case of difficulty, direct from BRF using the order form on page 111.

A Heart to Listen

Becoming a listening person in a noisy world

Michael Mitton

Listening has become a lost art in a world that is growing ever noisier, more superficial and more stressed. Too many of us have forgotten not only about listening to others but also about listening to God, to our own hearts, to our wider communities—and even to our planet. Without listening, how can we hope to gain wisdom, to build deep and truly caring relationships with all kinds of people, to share our faith?

This accessible book shows how, with God's help, we can re-learn the art of listening and in doing so become a source of help and healing for others and for ourselves. Biblical reflection is inter-woven with insights from the author's wide experience of listening ministry in the UK and abroad. Between each chapter are episodes of an intriguing story, which explores the book's themes through vividly imagined characters in a cross-cultural setting.

ISBN 1 84101 269 6   £7.99
Available from your local Christian bookshop or, in case of difficulty, direct from BRF using the order form on page 111.

Long Wandering Prayer

An invitation to walk with God

David Hansen

So many of us experience guilt and frustration about our prayer lives. We want to experience God's presence, to grow towards interceding, meditating and worshipping as earnestly as the 'prayer warriors' and saints that we read about. When we try, however, our thoughts are distracted and we can end up feeling bored and even irritated by the whole exercise.

In this book, author David Hansen offers the imaginative solution of 'wandering prayer': literally wandering in the countryside, along a beach or simply through the neighbourhood where we live—in the presence of God. As we wander, our thoughts can flow freely—speaking to God about whatever pops into our head, or pausing to reflect on whatever is before us, 'considering the lilies' as Jesus told us to do. Is our drive to control our minds in prayer—to focus on one thing or stick to one list—actually a way of hiding from God?

ISBN 1 84101 026 X £6.99
Available from your local Christian bookshop or, in case of difficulty, direct from BRF using the order form on page 111.

Transforming the Ordinary

Bible meditations for the everyday

John Henstridge

Like John Henstridge's first book, *Step into the Light* (BRF, 2000), this book is a series of prayer meditations based around Bible passages. The focus of *Transforming the Ordinary* is on helping us build awareness of God into the variety and ordinariness of our daily routines.

From celebrating a birthday to being stuck in a queue of traffic, the 30 meditations cover a range of familiar experiences and events, showing how we can learn, whatever our circumstances, to tune our hearts and minds into God's presence, there with us. The meditations can be used by individuals for their own personal prayer time, but the introduction also suggests ways of making use of them in a group setting.

ISBN 1 84101 316 1 £6.99
Available from your local Christian bookshop or, in case of difficulty, direct from BRF using the order form on page 111.

Quiet Spaces

Prayer interludes for busy women

Patricia Wilson

The intimate relationship with God you've yearned for is well within your grasp, despite the chaos of juggling multiple roles, deadlines and commitments. This book can help you to use even a few stray minutes as an opportunity for a 'prayer interlude', calming the mind and listening for God's still, small voice in the midst of the tumult around you.

Each 'prayer interlude', which can be completed in as little as five minutes, offers a calming passage from the Psalms, a prayer meditation, a thought from the words of Jesus, and an exercise to help readers as they go back into the busyness of the day.

ISBN 1 84101 339 0 £5.99
Available from your local Christian bookshop or, in case of difficulty, direct from BRF using the order form on page 111.

Along the Discipleship Road

Following Jesus today

Jay Colwill

By choosing to follow Jesus, setting off on the road of discipleship, we embark upon an adventure that will challenge us and take us into unknown territory. Along the way we will surely face all kinds of 'hills', times of struggle that present us with a stark challenge: do we press on, growing in strength and determination, or do we give up and turn back?

This book explores what we can learn from the stories of some of Jesus' disciples: Andrew, Peter, James, Mary Magdalene, Thomas and Matthew. Their experiences, their triumphs and failures of faith and, above all, their relationship with Jesus offer us help and guidance as we seek to follow him as disciples today.

ISBN 1 84101 401 X £6.99
Available from your local Christian bookshop or, in case of difficulty, direct from BRF using the order form on page 111.

ORDER FORM

REF	TITLE	PRICE	QTY	TOTAL
054 5	Driven Beyond the Call of God	£7.99		
335 8	A Fruitful Life	£6.99		
269 6	A Heart to Listen	£7.99		
026 X	Long Wandering Prayer	£6.99		
316 1	Transforming the Ordinary	£6.99		
339 0	Quiet Spaces	£5.99		
401 X	Along the Discipleship Road	£6.99		

POSTAGE AND PACKING CHARGES						
Order value	UK	Europe	Surface	Air Mail	**Postage and packing:**	
£7.00 & under	£1.25	£3.00	£3.50	£5.50	**Donation:**	
£7.01–£30.00	£2.25	£5.50	£6.50	£10.00	**Total enclosed:**	
Over £30.00	free	prices on request				

Name _____ Account Number _____

Address _____

_____ Postcode _____

Telephone Number _____ Email _____

Payment by: ☐ Cheque ☐ Mastercard ☐ Visa ☐ Postal Order ☐ Maestro

Card no. ☐☐☐☐ ☐☐☐☐ ☐☐☐☐ ☐☐☐☐

Expires ☐☐ ☐☐ Security code ☐☐☐ Issue no. ☐☐☐

Signature _____ Date _____

All orders must be accompanied by the appropriate payment.

Please send your completed order form to:
BRF, First Floor, Elsfield Hall, 15–17 Elsfield Way, Oxford OX2 8FG
Tel. 01865 319700 / Fax. 01865 319701 Email: enquiries@brf.org.uk

☐ Please send me further information about BRF publications.

Available from your local Christian bookshop.   BRF is a Registered Charity

brf

Resourcing your spiritual journey

through...

- Bible reading notes
- Books for Advent & Lent
- Books for Bible study and prayer
- Books to resource those working with
  under 11s in school, church and at home

- Quiet days and retreats
- Training for primary teachers
  and children's leaders
- Godly Play
- Barnabas RE Days

For more information, visit the **brf** website at **www.brf.org.uk**